Betterway Coaching Kids Series

# YOUTH BASEBALL
## THE GUIDE FOR COACHES & PARENTS

Betterway Coaching Kids Series

# YOUTH BASEBALL

REVISED & UPDATED!

## THE GUIDE FOR COACHES & PARENTS

*2nd Edition*

*John P. McCarthy, Jr.*

**BETTERWAY BOOKS**
CINCINNATI, OHIO

**Youth Baseball: The Guide for Coaches and Parents**. Copyright © 1996 by John McCarthy, Jr. Printed and bound in the United States of America. All rights reserved. No part of this book may be reproduced in any form or by any electronic or mechanical means including information storage and retrieval systems without permission in writing from the publisher, except by a reviewer, who may quote brief passages in a review. Published by Betterway Books, an imprint of F&W Publications, Inc., 1507 Dana Avenue, Cincinnati, Ohio 45207. (800) 289-0963. Second edition.

Other fine Betterway Books are available from your local bookstore or direct from the publisher.

00  99  98  97  96     5  4  3  2  1

**Library of Congress Cataloging-in-Publication Data**

McCarthy, John P.
   Youth baseball : the guide for coaches and parents / by John P. McCarthy,
Jr.—2nd ed.
     p.   cm. — (Betterway coaching kids series)
   Rev. ed. of: A parent's guide to coaching baseball. c1989. Includes index.
   ISBN 1-55870-398-5
   1. Baseball for children—Coaching. I. McCarthy, John P., Parent's guide to
coaching baseball. II. Title. III. Series.
GV880.4.M37   1995
796.357'62—dc20                            95-38878
                                             CIP

Edited by David Tompkins
Interior and cover designed by Sandy Conopeotis Kent
Cover photographs by Superstock
Interior illustrations by Lee Woolery

---

Betterway Books are available at special discounts for sales promotions, premiums and fund-raising use. Special editions or book excerpts can also be created to specification. For details contact: Special Sales Manager, Betterway Books, 1507 Dana Avenue, Cincinnati, Ohio 45207.

*To Linda, To Jackie, Michelle and Joey, to Kris and John Connor,
and to kids everywhere. Why I coach, why I am.*

*Special thanks to my photo models,
all-stars Joe McCarthy, Chris and Scott Demarest,
and the beautiful Jaime Capodiferro and Jaclyn Barton.*

# TABLE OF CONTENTS

# PREFACE

"What's he doing wrong?" The expression on Dave's face was dead serious, very concerned. I could hear the frustration in his voice. His son was ten years old. As a nine-year-old the season before, he had not gotten a hit, not one. Now, a few weeks into the new season, he was still not hitting. Dave pleaded, "It's really beginning to bother him. What can I do?"

I can't tell you how many times I've been asked these questions. And why not? Baseball is our most popular sport, and most parents want their kids to have fun with it, to do well. And some just don't want to be embarrassed in front of other parents.

The trouble with baseball's popularity is that a lot of coaches are needed, but very few are trained or knowledgeable. When I started twenty years ago, I knew nothing about coaching. Sure, I played baseball as a kid, and softball later on, but I knew nothing about coaching. Very few parents do when they volunteer to coach a team. Fortunately they do volunteer, but often they either don't know the basics or don't know how to coach them.

I went to the bookstore for some help, but most books were about big league baseball, written by big league experts. Coaching eight-, nine-, ten-year-old kids is completely different. Their needs are different. Big league coaches only deal with yesterday's youth baseball all-stars. They have no idea how to get a below average ten-year-old to hang in there. I remember wishing that there was a good book for parents and parent-coaches, one that better understood the special needs of children and that a parent could easily understand.

After all, parents are the ones who most influence whether a boy or girl will improve and stay with the game. That's right, we parents! We decide not to drive them to practice and, if the field is too far away, they don't play . . . maybe never play. Or, when sign-up time comes and they are a bit hesitant, our lack of support will end the question. On the other hand, if we decide to get up and throw a few pitches to our kids at an early age, it just may be that one day we have a ballplayer in the family. Most important, it is the parent who can help a kid to believe that he or she is a hitter and that hitting baseballs is easy and fun. By knowing a few basics, you can help mold a good bat swing, or at least prevent bad habits from developing. I've seen some bad habits take years to fix.

In today's youth baseball circles, parents have gotten a bad reputation. I chatted with a lifelong friend of my father's about this book. "Uncle Load" was always a good athlete and spent his later years coaching and administering youth sports. He laughed and told me, "Jackie, when it comes to parents there are two rules. The first rule is 'No parents,' and the second rule is 'Remember the first rule.' " In fact, when the subject comes up in conversation, people say, "Yeah, too bad about the way parents act—ruins everything."

Then it occurred to me that in all my years of coaching, I rarely had a parent problem. I figured it must be because I involved parents from the start. I got them directly involved with helping with the coaching. I'd tell them what to do and what to look for. They became knowledgeable, part of the team, and best of all, they learned how to coach their children on their own.

I'm not saying that just being supportive is not enough. It is more than many kids get from their folks. But you can go further if you want to, much further. This book gives you that option. It will give you enough to be a pretty decent coach if you want to be one, but it also will give you enough background just to help your child improve and hang in there. Whatever you do, it's going to make a difference. You will feel like a better parent, and your son or daughter will become a better ballplayer. Best of all, you and your child will become friends, just from playing together.

I coached my older son in Little League for six years. Then, after a six-year stint as coach of my daughter's soccer team, I returned to baseball to coach my younger son. I've also coached basketball.

Over the years I've learned a great deal about kids and parents. I've also learned lots of hints, tips and gimmicks on how to get kids going, get them to improve. These tips are all here in this book. They work! All of the teams I have coached have been winning teams, including several championship teams. My baseball teams were always known for their hitting. Not that I emphasize winning. I don't. I emphasize confidence, improvement and team spirit. These things lead to winning.

I'm convinced that there is a way to get every single kid going if he wants to, to get him feeling good about his ability. That's why I coach, that's why I wrote this book.

# Chapter One

# RULES OF THE GAME

## WHAT'S BASEBALL?

To a wide-eyed four-year-old, baseball has nothing to do with rules. It all begins with Dad or Mom pitching the ball. After what seems like a million swings and misses, suddenly contact is made and the universe erupts in shouts, bells and whistles. The child knows to run, somewhere, and then get back to home base before getting caught. That's baseball to the four-year-old, and if you think about it, that's the essence of baseball to all of us. It's a simple game: hit, run, get home.

After a while, that youngster starts to hang around the lot or field where the big shot six- to eight-year-olds play, with their fancy Little League or teeball hats. He or she may get a chance to run down some foul balls. One day the older kids find themselves a few players short and ask the rookie to play right field. And so, a baseball player is born. It's a rite of passage.

The sandlot game has remained simple. No umps, no walks, put the ball over the plate, ties go to the runner. It was a simple game in the early days of organized baseball, from the Civil War era up to the forming of the professional leagues before the turn of the twentieth century. Competition has since forced the development of more rules, to lessen heated disputes. But the love affair between people and baseball has much to do with its simplicity, and so it's still very much the game of that wide-eyed four-year-old.

There are some basics you must know. If you want detailed information, write to Little League Baseball, P.O. Box 3485, Williamsport, PA 17701, and ask for a copy of the official Little League rules. There are many excellent organizations for youth baseball. I refer to Little League since I coached it for nearly twenty years and find their rules very good. If your local club is affiliated with another organization, ask the president for a set of rules. I've also included a glossary of terms at the end of the book so you can start learning to speak the language of baseball.

## The Game

Baseball is a game where players use a bat to hit pitched balls onto a field of play. When a batter gets a *hit*, he or she then tries to run around a diamond-shaped *infield* touching each of four bases without being tagged out. Upon touching *home base*, the player scores a *run*. The team with the most runs at the end is the winner.

The defense tries to get players *out* before they score. They do so by retrieving the batted ball and then tagging the runner with it or by tagging a base toward which a runner is forced to advance (I'll deal with this concept of *forced outs* in more detail later). While touching a base, a player is *safe*. However, he is forced to advance to the next base if runners behind him must advance to his base.

Teams alternate on offense and defense. The game is divided into nine innings. An inning is played when each team has had a chance to bat. Once one team has made three outs in its half-inning, the next team gets *up at bat*. If the score is tied after nine innings, the game continues until an inning ends with one team ahead.

An out occurs when the batter gets three *strikes*; that is, the batter fails to hit the ball safely with three swings. A strike is also charged by the *umpire* when a batter fails to swing at a good pitch or if the ball is hit into foul territory. Additionally, a batter is out if a hit ball is caught by a defender before it touches the ground. Finally, outs are made, as noted above, when a runner is tagged between bases or when a player with the ball touches a base to which the runner must advance.

A player must advance to first base after hitting a fair ball that touches the ground before being caught. The batter may advance to first base with a *walk* if the pitcher throws the ball outside the *strike zone* four times. Normally, the player may advance to second, third and home base at her own risk and may *steal* the next base if she can get there without being tagged. However, once a player is on base, she must advance if another hit ball touches the ground and runners behind her must advance. When a player is safe on a base, the next batter may *get up*. Nine players are allowed to each team on the field at once.

## FIELD DIMENSIONS AND GENERAL RULES

A Little League field is small compared to big league fields. Players up to twelve years old play on a field about two-thirds the size of a big league field. (See figure 1-1.) Little League bases are 60 feet apart, about the same distance as on an adult softball field. In the professional leagues, the bases are a long 90 feet apart. Kids move to the 90-foot length at thirteen to fourteen years of age. This is usually a difficult adjustment. Some leagues move thirteen-year-olds to a 75-foot base to ease the transition a bit.

The pitcher pitches from a rubber mat, the front of which is 46 feet from the back point of home plate, as opposed to 60 feet 6 inches in the big leagues. In the early days of baseball, the pros pitched from 46 feet. It was a gentleman's game then, and pitches were underhand. When competition increased the speed of pitching in the 1880s, the mound was pushed back to its current spot. Little League fences are usually up to 200 feet from home plate, while professional league fences average about 350 feet. Often, fields for the youngest kids have no fences, so on a hot summer day a hard grounder can roll a mile on the baked ground.

The distance from home plate to the backstop is optional. Young players need a close backstop since the catchers will let many pitches go by. There is much stealing on these passed balls, and local rules often try to reduce the stealing, which can tend to dominate the game. The backstop at Yankee Stadium is 82 feet behind home plate; at Boston's Fenway Park it's only 60 feet, which is one of several reasons why Fenway is such a great hitter's park.

### Your Local Club

How children get placed onto the teams varies from town to town. Call a club official if you need to know this information. For players under age nine or ten, the teams usually are put together by the club officials. They call kids to a "tryout" where each is rated on a point scale. Then they try to give each team the same number of above and below average players. The officials do their best, but you never know until the umpire says "play ball" how well a kid can or will do.

At the nine- or ten-year-old level, the coaches usually get together and draft their teams just like in the pros. They have the kids' last

FIGURE 1-1

## REGULATION LITTLE LEAGUE FIELD

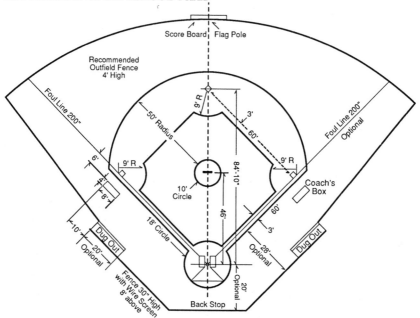

Official Little League field layout. All dimensions are compulsory unless marked "Optional."

year's ratings and their own notes. More experienced coaches, or ones like me who coach several sports, usually know the best talent. We draw lots to see who goes first and then go in rotation.

Little League has no rule requiring that every player get into the game, but nearly all clubs have a local rule requiring at least one "at bat" and two defensive innings. Games last for six innings. Some clubs require the coach to bat every player at the game in rotation, particularly in younger age groups. Check with your local board and get a copy of the rules concerning your club. Some clubs follow official Little League rules (which I prefer); others are independent and make up their own. If a coach violates these rules, particularly as to playing time, a parent should talk to him or call the club president.

## Batting Rules

A batter must stand in the batter's box. This is a 3 feet, 8 inch by 8 feet, 8 inch box on either side of the plate, starting 27½ inches

FIGURE 1-2
## REGULATION BATTER'S BOX

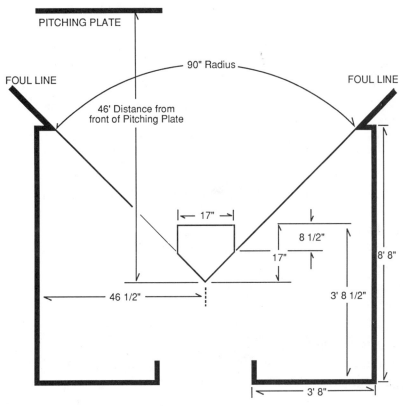

Official Little League layout of batter's box and compulsory dimensions.

behind the back tip of the plate and set 6 inches away from the side of the plate. A batter must be entirely inside the box while hitting the ball. Often, youth baseball fields are not "lined," and there is only an imaginary batter's box. I like to tell kids to stand as far back in the batter's box as the ump will allow. Using the whole 27½ inches gives the batter a split second more to see the ball, and it seems to shrink the strike zone. As noted, the batter's box ends 4 inches away from the side of the plate. A batter who crosses that line, especially by stepping on or in front of the plate when he swings, is out upon hitting the ball. (See figure 1-2.)

The *strike zone* is the area over home plate from the batter's knees to his armpits when he assumes a natural batting stance. If any part of a pitched ball passes through this area, the batter will be charged with a strike. (See figure 1-3.) Three strikes are an out. Strike zones often vary by umpires, and this is the source of most arguments in baseball. The strike zone has varied widely in the pros, with the upper part of the zone moving up and down over the years from the neck to the waist. A pitch outside the strike zone is called a *ball*. Four balls in one at bat entitles the batter to go to first base, called a *walk*. It kills me when a kid gets three balls, and then the coaches or parents start yelling, "A walk is as good as a hit," or "Swing only if it's good." Sure, with a 3-0 count (3 balls, no strikes) I agree. With 3 balls the batter has a good chance to earn a free base and should try to do so. Other than that we should always encourage a child to hit. There are times when a walk is a good idea, but it galls me to see a kid up who is obviously struggling and to hear people encouraging him to look for a walk so he can get on base. It may be good for those who think winning is important, but the message to the kid is, "Take a walk, kid, because we don't have much faith in your bat." If you don't have faith in him, he'll never find it!

## Fair and Foul Balls

A runner advances to first base, or beyond, upon a batted ball that lands in fair territory. The foul territory is the area outside the two foul lines. The foul lines run along the first and third baselines and extend out to the boundaries of the field, usually a fence. A foul ball is a batted ball that lands in foul territory. A foul tip is a ball nicked by the bat. If the catcher catches a foul tip on the third strike, the batter is out.

Here are the basic "fair or foul" rules:

- A ball that touches a foul line is still fair.
- A batted ball that passes first or third base landing in fair territory is a fair ball.
- A batted ball that touches in fair territory and then rolls foul before it gets to first or third base is a foul ball as soon as the fielder retrieves it.
- A batted ball that touches in fair territory and rolls foul after it passes any part of first or third base, even it it just grazes the

FIGURE 1-3
# THE STRIKE ZONE

Little League Rule 2.00: The strike zone is that space over home plate that is between the batter's armpits and the top of the knees when the batter assumes a natural batting stance. The umpire shall determine the strike zone according to the batter's usual stance when that batter swings at a pitch. When any part of the ball passes through any part of the strike zone a strike is called.

outside corner of the base, is a fair ball.

- If a player touches the ball in fair territory and then it goes foul, it is a fair ball. Misunderstandings as to this rule are usually good for a groan or two from parents during a game!

When a batter hits a ball that lands in foul territory, it is a strike unless the batter already has two strikes. Then it doesn't mean anything. There is no limit to the number of foul balls that may be hit. A foul pop-up may be caught in the air for an out. Runners then may tag up (touch their respective bases) and advance to the next base.

## Baserunning Rules

A runner is *forced* and must advance to the next base if she is on first base or if the bases behind her are filled and a hit ball touches fair ground. So if a runner is on first, she must get to second; if runners are on first and second, both must advance, and so forth. However, if a runner is on second, and no one is on first, then she

FIGURE 1-4

# THE FORCE PLAY

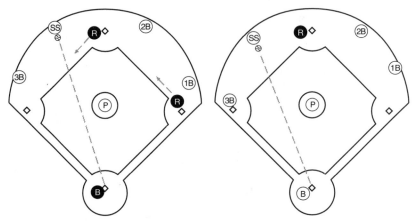

The runners on first and second are "forced" and must try to advance to the next base. They are out if any fielder touches that next base with the ball in hand before the runner arrives. The runner on second is not forced and may stay safely on the base in this instance.

is not forced and can stay on that base if it would be dangerous to try to advance (for example, on a ground ball hit toward third base). (See figure 1-4.)

If the ball is hit up in the air, the runner should not advance too far until the ball is caught or missed. If the ball is caught in the air, the runner must get back to his base before the ball can be thrown there or risk being *doubled-up*, meaning that both he and the batter are out. After a fly ball is caught, then the runner may tag up and advance. This often happens with a runner at third when a fly ball is caught deep in the outfield. The runner can usually tag third base and get home before the throw gets to the catcher.

Running into or obstructing a fielder trying to make a play or moving in a manner to hinder or distract a batter is called *interference*. In the first instance the runner is out and other runners return to the last base they touched. The ball is dead. In the latter the umpire warns the fielder to stop. If a fielder interferes with a runner, it is called *obstruction*.

The *infield fly* rule prevents infielders from intentionally dropping a pop-up to get a double play. The rule is that if the ball can

FIGURE 1-5

## THE INFIELD FLY RULE

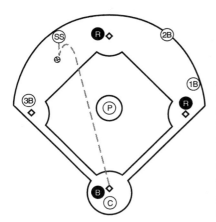

A complicated rule. If runners are on first and second, or bases are loaded, with no outs or one out, and a catchable infield pop-up is hit that could be caught with ordinary effort, then the runners are not forced if the fielder drops the ball. The batter is automatically out. The idea is to prevent fielders from intentionally dropping the ball, perhaps for an easy double play.

be caught by an infielder with ordinary effort, when there are runners on first and second or bases are loaded, with none or one out, the batter is automatically out and runners can tag up and advance at their own risk. (See figure 1-5). If the ball is dropped, the runners need not advance. Many Little League umpires do not use this rule. I think they just forget to call it or don't understand it.

Players are allowed to steal a base under certain conditions. Because the distance between bases is so short, runners are not allowed to take a lead (step off the base). They can leave the base when the pitched ball reaches the batter. Local rules sometimes prohibit stealing completely or prohibit stealing home.

If a batted ball hits a runner, if the runner interferes with a fielder, or if he doesn't slide into a base when the fielder at the base has the ball, he is out.

A runner who leaves the base before the pitch reaches the batter must go back. He is not automatically out. If the ball is hit, the runner must go back to the base, or to the next unoccupied base.

## Tie Games

Tie regulation games that are halted by the umpire due to weather, curfew or lack of light are resumed at the same point where they were stopped, if four innings have been completed. If one team is ahead at that time, or if the home team is ahead or tied after three and a half innings, it is a regulation game. If a game has not reached four innings, or three and a half innings with the home team losing, it is declared *no game*, and all scores are erased. The game is played over.

# Chapter Two

# HITTING

Hitting is the essence of baseball, and it's definitely the most fun. An old ballplayer once told me, "Defense is something you have to do while you are waiting to get up at bat again." Sure, fielding, running and throwing are big parts of the game, no doubt about it, but hitting is "numero uno."

Anyone who has ever hit a home run, or seen a loved one hit one, knows what I mean. For a moment everyone is breathless, watching the ball shudder as it fights wind currents against the sky, and then, as it floats down, all eyes straining to see if it will make the fence, the quiet moment of awe shatters under the roar erupting from the crowd. So, when it comes to skills, hitting is where it all starts.

Many coaches, especially big league coaches, will tell you that you either have it as a hitter or you don't. They will quote statistics showing that a player's average is generally highest early in his pro career, suggesting that there is usually little or no improvement from year to year. Well, that may be true for the big leagues, maybe even college, and perhaps high school (though I doubt it). But it is absolutely dead wrong for children. Kids can improve tremendously. I've seen it countless times. I've also seen kids get much worse. This tells me one thing loud and clear: Coaching helps, and parents count. Coaching can make the difference.

## CONFIDENCE: YA GOTTA BELIEVE!

This is the most important concept in this whole book. If hitting is the life of baseball, then confidence is its soul. If you can help your players get to the point where they *believe* they are good hitters, so they expect to hit the ball when they get up, then you have planted a seed whose growth cannot be denied. The kid at bat should be thinking about where the ball will go, not whether he or she will hit it.

You have to tell kids that they are already hitters. There is a hitter inside each one, maybe waiting to come out, maybe needing some help, some instruction, some experience, but definitely a hitter. At my first practice every year, that's just what I do. I tell my players they are hitters, I have them say it, I keep saying it. Sports psychologists say positive affirmation works. I have twenty years of coaching experience and have seen it work countless times. I make a fuss when someone makes good contact with the ball. The sound or "crack" of a well-hit ball is distinctive. I point it out to the kids, and pretty soon everybody is listening for it, everyone is trying to make that sound.

It's not a lie, not even a fib, not at the Little League level. All kids are hitters. Hitting is easy at the young ages: When the ball comes in more slowly, it's natural. The problems come when fear or doubts interfere with the positive attitude. Never, never, never criticize a player, or your child if you are a parent, in a way that tells her she is not a hitter. If you do, she may never become the hitter she already is. Just say, "You are a hitter, I know you are. We're almost there. It's coming. Ya gotta believe!" Then when it does come (and it will), when she swings the bat nicely or makes good contact (the first sign of improvement), you let the whole world know about it. Make that kid feel proud and confident, and her ability will blossom like a whole field of flowers.

One season I had a ten-year-old boy named Matt on the team. I had coached him as an eight-year-old and drafted him back because I liked him. This boy was motivated. He wanted to be a good hitter in the worst way. He had a tough season the year before, and he was having similar troubles early in this season—swinging too hard, trying too hard. He would strike out and start crying.

I told him it was OK to cry, no problem. It just showed how much he wanted to hit, and that was fine. I kept telling him that he was a hitter, that it would come, it was just around the corner. "Just relax a bit, Matt, control your energy. Swing with confidence. It'll come." And it did by midseason. The hits came and with them a smile you could float on and a gleam in his mother's eye that sparkled like sunshine. He really expected to hit the ball, and when that happens the hits will follow.

The worst problem with kids who are not hitting is often not their style of swinging; that's usually easy to fix. The main problems are fear and doubt. The two feed off each other. First, kids may be afraid that they will get hit by the pitcher. This occurs at about age eight or nine, when kids start pitching. The fear causes a defensive swing or stepping back until they can't even reach the ball. Then, after many hitless at bats, self-doubt takes over. They think they can't do it. They become afraid of being embarrassed in front of friends and parents. Now they have three problems: fear, self-doubt and a lousy swing. You have to face these problems head on. Tell a fearful batter he can do it, that it's easy, that he's a hitter, and that improvement is going to come as sure as the morning sun. Ya gotta believe!

Start with just a spark of confidence, then mold a good swing from that. It's natural to hit as long as the kid isn't fighting himself. If your players are to believe in themselves, *you have to believe in them*! Get rid of the negatives, focus on the positive, and things will happen the way they are supposed to happen. Good hitters think it's easy to hit; ask them, they are the ones who know!

## HITTING, HITTING, HITTING
### Practice, Practice, Practice

If confidence is the soul of baseball, then repetition is its backbone. I've had many winning teams in baseball and the main reason is lots of hitting practice. Emphasize hitting! I remember telling one parent after his nine-year-old was swinging the bat nicely, "He has a nice swing, now he just needs to hit a few thousand balls." Too often parents just go out and play catch with the child. No problem, but remember that hitting should also be emphasized.

The more a boy or girl practices hitting, the better he or she is going to be, especially at Little League age. Somebody has to pitch to them, practice with them. This is where parents come in. Tell the parents on your team to get a couple of balls and throw to their kids. Using several balls will save time chasing after them, unless you have an eager second child for that task. I have a whole bucket of balls that I use.

Tell mom or dad to pitch to the child at home. Tell them not to worry about how well they can pitch—they will improve too! Throw the ball close at first, from 25 to 35 feet away if that initially helps control. If the child is not making contact at that distance, move in until the right distance is found. Move back to 46 feet when you can. For kids younger than nine, 35 feet or less is fine: from nine onward you want to get to 46 feet as soon as possible.

Make it fun! When I did it with my son Joey, I had a marker on the field for the farthest distance he hit a ball on a fly that day. Have him try to hit to different fields—right, center and left. Twenty to thirty pitches is OK: more is better. Mickey Mantle's father used to pitch to him every day while his brother chased down the balls. Repetition works, guaranteed! It works not only to get the mechanics refined, but it also helps with body chemistry, as chapter seven on the psychology of coaching baseball discusses in detail.

Another great idea is to take your child to an area batting cage. I used them all the time fifteen years ago. Now a lot of teams do it. In some areas indoor cages are springing up, and they are great for rainy days. They usually have a slow and medium speed cage for children. First watch for a minute and pick out the best speed. Often the manager can adjust speed to accommodate different ages. Eleven- and twelve-year-olds should hit a 45-mph pitch. Start slow and build up speed. It's about a dollar-fifty for twenty balls. Four or five dollars worth, sixty balls, is a thorough workout, and is about the most you should do. I'd tell the kids to offer to wash and wax mom's car for the money. Also, kids should take their own bats if they have one—the grips are often lousy on batting cage bats. A batter's glove is also very useful, since the hand can get sore from a good workout. Batting cages have helmets—ask for one. Take a break after each twenty balls and talk about the swing, or watch other batters. The idea is to do a lot of hitting—that's the key to it all. Have her take swings lefty (if she is righty) and bunt a few, too. Give a holler when she makes good contact. Take some swings yourself!

## THE BASICS

In a game a dozen years ago, an eight-year-old got up to the plate. You could see that he was uncomfortable and didn't really know what to do. He chopped at the first pitch for a strike, and his coach started yelling, "C'mon, hit the ball, hit the ball." The next pitch came in, and the boy missed it by more than a foot. Again the coach started screaming, "Hit the ball, c'mon, hit the ball." Finally, the kid turned in frustration and shrieked to his coach, "All right, but how? I'm trying, but how?"

I walked up to the boy. At that age the coaches all helped each other, and I knew his parents. "No problem, Scott, just keep your eye on it. Watch it leave the pitcher's hand, and watch it until it's in front of you, right over the plate. Don't take your eyes off it." On the next pitch, he hit the ball. He popped out, but he hit the ball. After he turned to go to the dugout, he flashed a big grin at me— it made my day!

Saying general things like "hit the ball" is not helpful. Yell out some of the basics like "see the whole ball," "keep your head down," "swing with confidence," "keep your hands up," "hard bat," or "don't drop your right shoulder." These things are helpful. The next sections discuss such specifics in detail.

It's a big help to be supportive, to raise confidence, and to practice with the kids. If that's all you do, it's still a great help. But the detailed knowledge of some hitting basics—working with young players on the mechanics of the stance, the swing—will reap immediate and permanent rewards. There is clearly a science of hitting, and those who can teach it will see great improvement quickly in their players. So, let's get on to it.

## Keep Your Eye on the Ball

*Important!* Most kids don't usually "see" the pitch until it's about one-third of the way to them. Then they start their swing, and don't really see the ball for the last 5 to 10 feet. This means that they only see the ball for a little more than half of the time it's in flight, less than a split second. There's no way a child is going to hit the ball if he doesn't see it, not hit it hard anyway. The most important thing you can say when you practice, or at a game when he is up, is simply, "Keep your eye on the ball! Watch it leave the pitcher's hand, all the way to the bat!" Make sure you read the section in chapter eight on how to improve vision.

There are a couple of hints you can consider. I remember when my eldest son, Jackie, was nine years old. There was a boy named Ray on our team, a big kid, very quiet, and not particularly sure of himself. But he had a big heart and wanted to play ball.

He hadn't gotten many hits during the season. He was tight when he swung, and he didn't swing often. During one game he had struck out a few times, and then he was up late in the game. The score was close so I had to get him to swing. I called "time out" from my third base coaching spot and went over to talk to him. I said, "Ray, you're a hitter, so I want you to do something for me. I want you to swing at every pitch. This pitcher is good and he'll get the ball over the plate. Also, I want you to see which way the ball is spinning as it comes toward you, and tell me after each pitch." Well, he missed the first pitch in the dirt, but took the second pitch over the center fielder's head. As he ran to first base (he watched the ball first for a full three seconds; everybody was screaming at him to run) he turned to me, raised his hand and pointed his finger, rotating it in a clockwise direction. He was telling me which way the ball was spinning! We had found a way to get him to look closely at the ball and he got a big hit. Of course, he was so long getting around the bases that he got tagged out at home (I *had* to send him!), but I don't think he ever knew it—everybody was cheering so loudly. His family moved after the season, and we got Christmas cards for a few years. My wife went back to college for some courses last year and guess who she had in one class—Ray, as big as a house!

Look at your player's eyes and head when he swings. If he lifts his head or turns it with his shoulders as he swings, he is not looking at the ball long enough. Tell him to try to see the ball while it's still in the pitcher's hand, so he can be sure to watch it from the start. He must also see the ball in front of him, over the plate, until the bat hits it. Tell him to keep his head still and try to see the bat hit the ball. He should be looking right down his arms, along the bat. He won't be able to actually see the bat hit it, but he'll watch the ball long enough to hit it.

So those are the three hints: Watch the ball leave the pitcher's hand, watch it closely enough to see it spin as it comes toward the plate, and try to see it hit the bat. Then tell him to run, because he will hit it!

## The Stance

The stance is the batting position assumed when waiting for the pitch. First of all, if you watch a pro baseball game, you will see eighteen different stances. Yankee old-timer Don Baylor liked to get close to the plate to pull the ball to left field. That's why he got hit by pitches so often. Pete Rose bent way forward so his head was right in the strike zone; he "saw" the ball very well, and that's why he is the all-time leader in hits. Many guys, like old-timer Rod Carew, point their bat back right at the ump, and they swing very level, slapping out a lot of singles—high batting average but no real power. Other guys wrap the bat around their heads. Reggie Jackson spread his legs wide; Stan Musial kept them close. Some plant the right foot back a bit, some the left. In 1986 Don Mattingly used to "pigeon toe" his back foot a bit, to get more power. For some reason he stopped in 1988, and he never had a great year slugging again. Mel Ott used to lift up his left foot so high when he swung that he looked like he was about to fall down.

The key to a stance is to let the batter be comfortable—this is one area where you give a young player *some* freedom to do it his way. I'm not saying that there isn't a "right" stance, and I'm going to tell you what it is. There are clearly some important "don'ts" I'll touch on. I'm just saying that hitting is less affected by the stance than by other things, so here is an area where you can allow room for some personal style. Kids are built differently, so different styles may be more comfortable than others.

At very young ages, children try to face you as you pitch the ball. It looks cute, but you must gently insist that they stand sideways. Second, young children tend to hold the bat right in front of the breastbone. So you need to move the bat farther back, near the right (for righties) shoulder, with the hands up and even with the shoulder. Once you've gone over the basics, tell the batter to "look like a hitter." Then, when he or she begins to lapse back into an improper stance, just repeat the phrase "look like a hitter" and watch that kid snap into a correct stance. The main thing in a stance is to keep the hands up and back a bit. At the very least make sure the batter does this.

Some coaches put way too much emphasis on stance. They can really screw up a kid, so much that the kid seems to forget how to swing at all. I've seen coaches do nothing but work on a kid's stance, and by the time they are done the kid holds the bat like a stone statue and swings as if stuck in concrete. It's OK to aim for the "correct" stance, just don't try too much at once. Work with one thing at a time, from the context of the child's present stance.

What is a "correct" stance? The following is for righties; do the opposite for lefties. (See figure 2-1).

1. Keep the feet a bit wider than shoulder distance apart. If the feet are close together you get more power, since you take a bigger stride toward the ball. However, this also means the body is lunging, so you lose some bat control. If the feet are spread wide, you get the opposite—less lunge, less power, but more control. Adjust to what's comfortable, what works best. The key is to feel balanced. Adjust so the legs feel balanced.

2. The left foot should never be past the plate, toward the pitcher. Usually, the farther the batter stands back in the batter's box toward the catcher the better. It gives the batter more time to see the ball and also shrinks the strike zone. Of course, if the pitcher is throwing a lot of low pitches, the batter has to move forward (closer to the pitcher) to meet the ball before it drops. The feet should be close enough to the plate so that the end of the bat covers the outside portion of the plate with a few inches to spare.

3. The right foot can be set even with the left, but preferably a few inches back behind the batter; the left or front foot should be closer to the plate. The back foot should be pointed straight ahead, or even pigeon-toed a bit for more power.

4. The weight should be on the balls of the toes, a bit more weight on the back foot. Sometimes I stick a glove or a bat under the right heel to keep it up so the weight is more on the toes. Flat-footedness is a no-no; it causes a jerky swing with less power and control. Again, stress balance.

5. Bend the knees a bit, as much as is comfortable. The idea is to be loose, to have the feeling of balance.

6. Also, bend forward from the waist a little bit. This helps the batter loosen up, keeps the weight forward on the balls of the toes, and gets the head closer to the strike zone to see the ball.

7. The hands should be together, an inch or so from the bottom of the bat. Make sure the bat is not too heavy. The pros today have gotten away from the big heavy bats used in the old days. The bats are still big, but the grips are thinned out. This allows them to whip

FIGURE 2-1

# THE STANCE—FRONT VIEW

It is essential for the coach to look at each part of a batter's stance to see if there are any flaws. Start at the feet and work upward point by point.

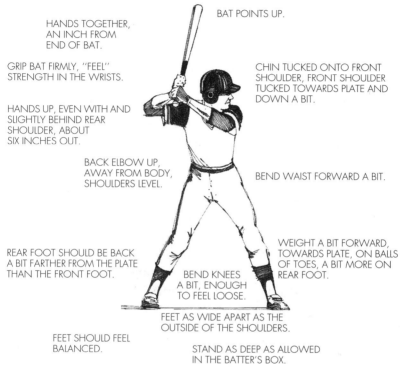

HANDS TOGETHER, AN INCH FROM END OF BAT.

GRIP BAT FIRMLY, "FEEL" STRENGTH IN THE WRISTS.

HANDS UP, EVEN WITH AND SLIGHTLY BEHIND REAR SHOULDER, ABOUT SIX INCHES OUT.

BACK ELBOW UP, AWAY FROM BODY, SHOULDERS LEVEL.

BAT POINTS UP.

CHIN TUCKED ONTO FRONT SHOULDER, FRONT SHOULDER TUCKED TOWARDS PLATE AND DOWN A BIT.

BEND WAIST FORWARD A BIT.

WEIGHT A BIT FORWARD, TOWARDS PLATE, ON BALLS OF TOES, A BIT MORE ON REAR FOOT.

REAR FOOT SHOULD BE BACK A BIT FARTHER FROM THE PLATE THAN THE FRONT FOOT.

BEND KNEES A BIT, ENOUGH TO FEEL LOOSE.

FEET AS WIDE APART AS THE OUTSIDE OF THE SHOULDERS.

FEET SHOULD FEEL BALANCED.

STAND AS DEEP AS ALLOWED IN THE BATTER'S BOX.

BE STILL. NO DANCING, NO WIGGLING BAT, NO WIGGLING HIPS. STILL BUT NOT STIFF.

the bat around very quickly. Bat speed is important, so have your players start off with a light bat.

It's possible, however, to have too light a bat. In 1989 I had a kid named Danny, big kid, who was having trouble making contact. His dad was helping me coach, and I told him the problem was mainly mechanical. One day at pregame batting practice, I told Danny to get a heavier bat. Then he started making contact! During the game he smashed a screaming double, went two for three and won the game. So, sometimes you have to experiment. Tell the kids to try different bats in batting practice. They will figure out pretty quickly what bat works for them, under your close guidance. Also, have them choke up a few inches if they need to be in complete control of the bat. Don't interlock fingers, even if the golfer in the family thinks it's a good idea.

8. The grip, holding the bat, should be firm, not quite a squeeze, but nice and firm. Tell the batter to "feel" the strength in the wrist and forearm through the fingers into the bat. There are different ways to place the hands in relation to each other. In the most normal grip, the largest finger bones of the fingers on both hands are in a line. The knuckles of each hand are lined up with the large mid-finger joints of the other hand. This grip gives both power and control. (See figure 2-2.) For more power, separate the wrists a bit more. The knuckles of the top hand are then directly above the largest finger bones of the lower hand. This draws in the forearms and shoulders for more power. (See figure 2-2.) For more control, you can use an open grip. Bring the wrists closer together. In the open grip, the large midfinger joints are lined up. This looser grip tends to give a lot more control, relying more on the wrist. It also gives more snapping wrist action and helps the batter make contact when contact is really needed. Choking up also leads to more bat control. A control grip uses more of the fingers. The power grip also relies mainly on fingers but also brings in the palm pads under the main knuckles. In any case, the bat hardly touches the bottom of the palm of the hand.

9. The hands should be kept up by the right shoulder, not lower than the top of the strike zone. I like to see the hands right in front of or just behind the right shoulder, about 4 to 6 inches out. Holding the bat too low is a part of the stance you *must change*—no choice, hands have to be up. But not too high, top of the shoulder maximum.

10. The bat should point up and back a bit toward the catcher. Make sure it's not wrapped back behind the head; there's no need for the top of the bat to travel farther than necessary. Some kids like to wrap it around the head or sit it on the shoulder; they must change this. The less distance the head of the bat has to drop to get to the top of the strike zone the better!

11. The right elbow should be up, away from the body but not so high as to be uncomfortable. This is important. Many kids will start the swing with that back elbow and the upper arm too close to the body. This can cause the whole right side to drop, causing

FIGURE 2-2

## GRIPS

Normal Grip: The large finger bones are lined up, knuckles and large finger joints are lined up.

Tight or Closed Grip: Separate wrists a bit more. Knuckles on top hand are over large finger joints on lower hand, and vice versa. Closed grip gives more power.

a golf-like uppercut swing, one of the more difficult problems to cure. Stop it early! The swing must be level, and one key to a level swing is hand and elbow position. The raised elbow keeps the shoulders level. A level swing has a much better chance of hitting the ball. This is one of the keys, and it must be emphasized. Make sure that the angle between the upper arm and the right side of the chest is 45 degrees or more.

12. The head should obviously be facing the pitcher, chin tucked in near the left shoulder. The left shoulder is tucked in a bit toward the plate. The eyes are focused on the spot where the pitcher will release the ball, at the top of his stretch. It's important to keep the head stationary (just as in golf).

13. Now the batter is ready. One more thing—the body must be still. Any unnecessary motion could cause the bat to move a millimeter from the spot where the eyes say the ball is. Being still also helps concentration. Some batters like to "dance," move their feet around or shake the bat. It may help their nerves, but it never helps the swing. Be still. Like a coiled snake, like a cat on its haunches, like a guided missile, waiting, ready to explode on the ball in one sharp, quick motion.

Talk about these ideas as you work with your players. Tell them to stay balanced. Get them thinking about these things, not worrying how well they are doing. Get their minds off themselves and onto the ball. Remember, be still but not stiff! (See figure 2-3.)

## The Swing

I have talked about the initial part of the swing, such as keeping the eye on the ball all the way to the bat, keeping loose and still, leaning forward and keeping the weight back on the balls of the toes of the back foot, keeping the bat pointed up and back a bit, keeping the wrists and forearms strong, and holding the bat firmly, right elbow away from the body, hands up. Now I will discuss the swing itself. (See figure 2-4.)

1. Get a good pitch. Another reason to keep the eyes on the ball is to be able to pick out a good pitch. This is a very important fundamental. Yell out, "Get a fat one." A ball out of the strike zone cannot be hit well and cannot be hit hard. High pitches pop up, low ones turn into weak grounders. Inside or outside pitches are usually hit foul. Most of the time it's just a swinging strike. Tell your batter to look for the good pitch, never let a good pitch go by because you don't get that many. When you pitch, talk about each pitch—was it a ball or a strike? In practice it's OK to swing at bad pitches (if they are at least close!) because it teaches bat control, but make sure the batter knows when the pitch is not in the strike zone. He will, eventually, be able to tell the difference before the ball is halfway to him. Talk about these concepts. A good pitch usually feels good.

2. Step into the pitch. The biggest fear kids have in batting is getting hit by the ball. (The second is fear of embarrassing themselves.) So a major problem with many kids is what we call "stepping into the bucket." (See figure 2-5.) They step away from the ball, toward third base, as they swing. This causes their body, and consequently the bat, to move out of the strike zone. No way they can hit anything except maybe an inside pitch.

This part of the swing is called the *stride*; it is a short 6- to 8-inch step toward the pitcher. The idea here is to get the body moving directly toward the pitcher, into the ball. The stride immediately

FIGURE 2-3
# IMPROPER STANCES

Face home plate, left leg too far back.

Hands are too low, and not back by shoulder.

Bat wrapped around head.

Stance too far forward, past plate.

FIGURE 2-3 (cont.)

# IMPROPER STANCES

Stiff-legged, weight on back of feet.

Shoulders not level.

Over-rotated, back to pitcher.

Weight too far forward.

FIGURE 2-3 (cont.)
# IMPROPER STANCES

Feet too close.

Hands too close to body.

Too close to plate.

Hands not together.

FIGURE 2-4
# THE SWING

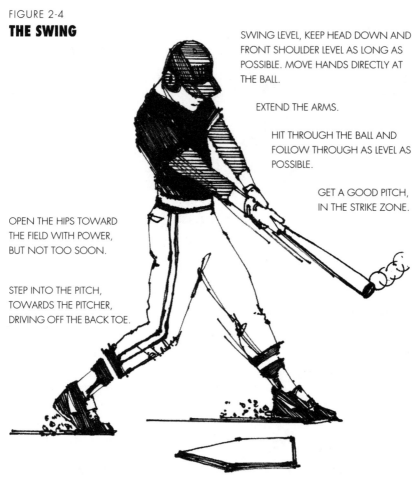

SWING LEVEL, KEEP HEAD DOWN AND
FRONT SHOULDER LEVEL AS LONG AS
POSSIBLE. MOVE HANDS DIRECTLY AT
THE BALL.

EXTEND THE ARMS.

HIT THROUGH THE BALL AND
FOLLOW THROUGH AS LEVEL AS
POSSIBLE.

GET A GOOD PITCH,
IN THE STRIKE ZONE.

OPEN THE HIPS TOWARD
THE FIELD WITH POWER,
BUT NOT TOO SOON.

STEP INTO THE PITCH,
TOWARDS THE PITCHER,
DRIVING OFF THE BACK TOE.

As with the stance, look at each part of the swing specifically.

follows a momentary shifting or rocking of the weight to the back foot. The batter should keep the weight back as long as possible to prevent striding too soon or lunging at the ball. Now your player is ready to begin the swing, a quick, powerful, balanced, exploding action. She must drive or push herself forward with the back foot, and lift or step the front foot toward the pitcher. The back foot pivots, allowing first the hips and ultimately the whole upper torso to turn. The front foot does not point toward the pitcher but just slides forward.

I remember a husky, freckle-faced redhead named Todd, who as a ten-year-old had a bad habit of stepping out. His dad said he had been doing it for two years. He was a good hitter, except he usually couldn't reach the ball after stepping back so far. So he struck out a lot. I had his father put a piece of 4x4 wood behind his feet in practice, and it worked. It took a while, but he settled down and started to become the hitter he was.

Some kids don't stride at all. Their swing is stiff and jerky, making it very hard to hit the ball squarely. (See figure 2-5.) One way to deal with this is to have your players take practice swings, without a pitched ball. Just step and swing, about fifty times a day. Tell them to pretend they see the ball coming toward them and step into the pitch and swing! It will loosen up their swing. Don't let them get sloppy. Do about twenty-five at first and build up to fifty quality swings. If it gets to be a habit, then they will do it naturally in a real situation. We used to get a bat in the living room and take some swings, talking about the stance and the swing. Try it (but move the lamps out of the way).

Remember, the idea is to get the body moving with the swing into the ball and to avoid stepping away from the ball.

3. Swing level. I remember a nine-year-old named Keith who loved to play ball and did it with his heart. But he had the worst swing I ever saw. It looked like he was hitting a golf ball out of a sand trap, a wild looping uppercut. First, if he hit the ball, it went straight up. Second, he missed a lot because such a swing requires more timing. The bat is moving upward and has to meet the ball at a single spot. A level swing can meet the ball anywhere over the plate. Third, such a swing causes the shoulders to tilt severely, and this moves the head up and takes the eyes off the ball. (See figure 2-5.)

I tried everything with Keith. I had him hold his hands higher and get his right elbow up more. His problem was in lifting the left elbow and shoulder and dropping the right side. I told him to try to chop down at the ball, like chopping a tree down. (By the way, these suggestions often do work, and you should always try them first.) Finally, I had no choice but to tell him to bat lefty. Kids usually will swing level from the opposite side but with less power. Keith still hit the ball well. The next year, his coach moved him back to righty, and time had softened the arc in his swing. Some things just need time. Keith will make the all-star team someday, but it's too bad that his bad habit held him back a few years.

The way to teach kids to swing level is to tell them to straighten out the left arm and move the hands directly toward the ball, on a straight line. Don't let the left elbow come out and up! Perceive the bat coming down to meet the ball rather than up into it. The bat will then also move on a straight line. As noted earlier, holding the hands up and keeping the shoulders level (don't drop the right side) also help a level swing.

Another problem behind an uppercut swing is lifting up the head. If this occurs, remind your player to keep the head down and still. I saw a coach recently put a glove on his batter's head to keep it from jerking out. The batter learned to keep the head still or the glove would drop before contact. It was a great idea!

` 4. Another key to a level swing is to make sure that the player doesn't "hitch." A hitch is a cocking motion that many players make with their hands just as they go into their swing. They move their hands down and up, instead of keeping them still and moving them straight out toward the ball. A hitch also takes time and causes a player to swing late at a fastball. Tell the batter to keep her hands still and move them outward only with the swing, directly at the ball. A backward hitch is better than an up-and-down one, but no hitch is best of all.

5. Open the hips. As noted earlier, the batter should keep the weight back and hips steady as long as possible. Then, just at the end of the stride and beginning of the swing, the hips turn or "open up" giving power, speed and torque to the swing. The hips ultimately open up completely, facing the pitcher.

6. Extend the arms. A tight, choppy swing, with the hands close to the chest, often goes along with stepping into the bucket. It's a defensive swing. Such a swing may suggest some self-doubt or concern about getting hit by the ball. It also is often found with a stance that puts the weight back on the heels, standing straight up instead of leaning forward at the knees and waist. One way to deal with it is to have the player stand farther from the plate during practice, to force him to bend forward, weight forward, and extend the arms fully at the point of contact. Tell him to "throw his hands out at the ball," and this will extend the arms.

Some kids just chop or slap at the ball. The idea is to hit *through*

FIGURE 2-5
## IMPROPER SWING

Too stiff, no stride, hips not open.

Uppercut swing—left elbow comes up and out, head comes up. Note also right hand came off bat.

Lunge—reaching for the ball too soon.

"Stepping into the bucket"—front leg steps toward third base.

the ball. Batters need to follow through with the swing, so the bat ends up all the way behind them. Try to hold the head down as long as possible, and keep the back foot down, on the toes, but not dragging.

## OTHER TIPS

If you have read this far, you know as much as you need about hitting to help your players or your son or daughter. Let's summarize, and if this seems repetitious, then I'm practicing what I preach, as I'll do a lot of repetition in this book.

• Be supportive generally—if you can't drive your child to practice, help him find some way to get there, make a phone call to another parent. If you are a coach and a kid has problems getting to practice that his parent can't or won't resolve, ask if a player nearby will pick him up.

• Be positive. She is a hitter already, she just has to believe that. Don't help her confirm her doubts about herself.

• Promote repetition. Tell parents to go out and pitch to their kids, or have a catch. If there are a few kids around, suggest they play ball. Get them organized into a game, help oversee it, pitch to them. Sometimes kids will argue for two hours about who is on what team or who is up first. You can help get them beyond that, get them on their way to doing it. When I pitch to my son Joey, I grab a bucket of balls and it takes only about ten or fifteen minutes to get thirty to forty swings. We go pick up the balls together.

### The Basics

Learn what to look for in a stance. Look at the placement of the feet, the knees, the hands. Is he standing too stiffly? Bend knees and waist to loosen up. Look at the swing. Is it level? Is he dropping his shoulder, elbow, hands, whole right side? Does he see the ball the whole way to the bat?

Don't push too hard, don't berate him if he doesn't feel like playing, just suggest it. Once he starts to improve, and he definitely will improve with your help, his desire to play will soar. Kids love to do something they feel good about. They love to have fun.

Here is another of my secrets, maybe my best one! When I pitched to my kids, Jackie, Sis and Joey, I did so while down on my right knee. (See figure 2-6.) I've been doing it this way for many, many years. I remember when I was a kid, my coach always seemed so tall, and the ball would be coming down on me from eight feet high. It was dropping fast, and I had to swing an uppercut to get a

FIGURE 2-6

## PITCHING ON ONE KNEE

The best tip I have! It brings an adult's pitch in lower and more level. That's me with my wife and son.

solid contact. When you pitch on a knee, the ball leaves your hand at the same height that a ten-year-old's does. It comes at your son or daughter in a much more level flight.

Now pitching from the knee might sound tough, and I guess it is, but I didn't notice. If the players are young, and you do it from 35 to 40 feet, you can develop some control. You have to have faith in practice for yourself if you are going to teach its value to someone else! If your players are older, eleven or twelve, don't get closer than 40 feet or you might wind up wearing the ball.

By the way, you don't need a catcher, just a backstop. And don't let another player or adult get back there without a face mask and other protection. A foul tip is hard to catch and may hit the face. You'll get used to the strike zone. If you have several balls, use them all, then go pick them up when you are out. This also helps to get many swings in a short period. I use about ten or fifteen balls. I get them as a coach and can build up a supply. I buy a box of twelve each year for myself. If your kid is under ten, the cheap cork balls are good enough. I've seen them on sale for a buck and a quarter. However, older kids bang them out of shape too quickly. One More Tip: Get something soft to kneel on—it makes it easier to be able to walk after practice. I use a catcher's chest protector. A small pillow is OK.

I think pitching on my knee has resulted in quality batting practice. Of all my secrets, I think this is the most effective. My teams always hit the ball, so something is working.

There are two other drills that are good, especially for parents who want to work one-on-one with their child and want to save having to chase balls. Your local sporting goods store will have a "ball on a string" that you whip around your head in a circular motion and then step toward your child, moving the ball into the strike zone. This is excellent practice for seeing the ball. A better drill is to stand to the side and lob the ball into the strike zone. The batter can stand facing the backstop (or a net), so the ball doesn't go far. Have him or her work on stance and hitting down on the ball—no pop-ups allowed! I'll discuss these drills in more detail in chapter six.

Batting tees are used in some pre-Little League clinics. I have mixed feelings about them. They teach a kid to swing a bit differently, since they don't need to worry about timing to meet a moving ball. Yet it does get the kids involved at a very young age—six or seven—and they are pretty much guaranteed to hit the ball. I've seen our local high school use them to work on form, so they can be quite useful. I always pitched to my kids, underhand if I had to, but the ball was moving. Try using a tee if you want, maybe combine it with pitching, depending on the age of your players.

Have you ever heard of pepper? It's an exercise they do in the big leagues where a coach will stand six feet from a couple of players and softly hit them grounders. They lob the ball back to the bat and he hits to someone else; you keep it moving and it develops reflexes. I do the reverse for batting. I get the kids up close with bats and they try to hit it softly to where I tell them—at my shoe, my knee, my glove. It's a great drill that builds confidence and a sense of contact with the ball.

A few words about equipment are in order. Little League starts in the spring, and it's often cold. The season starts early because vacations often begin right after school and, invariably, some kids have to leave then. Also, tournaments start then and the better players go to all-star teams. When it's cold, the bat stings the hands upon contact with the ball. A batting glove will eliminate the sting. Get one for each hand; cheap ones will do. If the player's winter gloves are not too thick, they will work, too. Even a pair of socks are better than nothing, although they will make the bat a bit slippery and harder to hold onto. Helmets are a must: Any hard hat or helmet will do. Spikes help give traction to the right foot as it drives the body toward the ball, but they are not essential for practice. Remember, use a light bat; don't fall into the trap of getting something so heavy it warps the swing.

## Switch Hitting

Not too many kids can switch hit. I guess it's tough enough to get good from one side. But when you watch the pros, half the team is platooned—righties facing lefties, and vice versa. The idea is that a righty can see the ball better if it comes from the outside, that is, the pitcher's left side. It starts out in front of the batter. Whereas when the pitcher is a righty, especially sidearm righty, the ball seems like it's starting from behind the batter. I really can't say I've emphasized switch hitting. I do have my kids bat lefty for a few pitches each at practices just so they can see what it feels like. I basically use the switched stance to give a kid a slightly different perspective, to change something a player is doing wrong.

When I was about eight or nine, we had just moved to the country, and I had never played baseball. I joined a team and couldn't hit the ball to save my life. Then one day, after what seemed like a million strikeouts, my coach told me to get up lefty. I don't know whether he had an idea or was just frustrated. But I got a hit the first time up. The new angle forced me to look at the ball better, somehow I saw it better (because the pitcher was righty?). I also swung more level. It felt awkward, and I had less power, but it worked.

## BUNTING

Bunting is a lost art in youth baseball. Very few coaches teach it, but I like to do some of it. I guess it's because the pitcher is so close to the batter (only 46 feet instead of 60 feet 6 inches as in the pros), and so he can get to the ball very quickly and throw the batter out. Nevertheless, it should be practiced.

FIGURE 2-7
# BUNTING

Turn to face the pitcher, feet balanced, head of bat up a bit, cradle mid-bat between thumb and forefinger, soft touch. Bottom hand can be choked up quite a ways for more control.

I remember a play-off game in 1986, nine-year-olds, and we needed a run to tie the score. We were facing the best pitcher in the league. He threw hard, and he threw strikes. The boy who was up could make contact, but he was small and couldn't get the ball out of the infield, not against that pitcher. The on-deck batter (the next batter up) was a very good hitter. So I told the batter to bunt and run like the dickens. It worked. He got on and my next batter tied the game with a shot in the gap.

When practicing bunting, tell the batters to turn and face the pitcher just as he pitches the ball. (See figure 2-7.) The batter should slide his right hand a third of the way toward the top. Keep the head of the bat high in the strike zone; you want to hit down on the ball. I also tell older players that they can slide the lower hand along the bat toward the middle. It makes the bat more flexible, but younger players may not be able to control the bat's recoil. When bunting, a player must concentrate on the ball more closely, watching its spin, then let the ball hit the bat. If he moves the bat toward the ball it will roll right to the pitcher, so he must just hold the bat firmly and let the ball hit the bat, even recoil the head of the bat back a bit. Tell your player to try to push it down the third base line softly and push off the back foot just as he does. Foot speed helps here—don't look back, just go for the base.

Well, that's it for hitting. Even if you only improve hitting, you'll have been a great help, because hitting is of primary importance. However, if you want your players to be really good at the other things they do while they are waiting to bat, then read on!

# Chapter Three

# FIELDING

To many ballplayers, defense is just "the thing you try to hit the ball over." Well, it's true that hitting is the essence of baseball, but teams rarely win without good defense. Unfortunately, defense is often the last thing kids learn. Many youth coaches hit grounders to kids and have outfielders shag fly balls, but not many know how to teach the basics. I'm not being critical of youth coaches, it's just that defense is the stepchild skill of this great game, and little quality time is spent on it at young ages. Coaches often figure a kid either has defensive skills or he doesn't.

As a result, a typical youth baseball scenario starts with an "easy out" ground ball, and soon players are throwing the ball all over the place. Scores are high with the younger kids because of poor defense.

Part of the problem is that there is never enough practice time. You get the kids for only a few hours a week. During the season the fields are often reserved for games, so there is very little practice opportunity. Practice fields are sometimes badly rutted, especially in springtime, and not good for defensive practice. That is where parents come in. Parents can teach their child some simple things, and as a coach I spend a lot of time talking to parents about how to help their child play better defense. Parents often want to help—they just need some good ideas on how. Substantial improvement in defensive play can come with some regular practice in the backyard.

Fielding is essentially catching and throwing. I'll address both skills generally. Chapter five discusses defense further from the perspective of each field position.

## CATCHING

The best way to begin learning how to catch, particularly at very young ages, is to do just that—have a catch. Every practice should begin with the kids having a catch to loosen up. You can't afford to waste a lot of time on such a basic skill as catching balls. So tell parents to get a couple of gloves and a ball, and go out at home with their child for a catch. This is important for kids who can't catch well at all.

At first, throw the ball softly back and forth. Start at a comfortable distance—15 to 25 feet. I've seen many parents, especially mothers who have had little experience with baseball, learn very quickly. Remember, if you practice you will improve too, so don't be bashful. It may be easier to use a tennis ball at first, or a rubber ball with a sponge-like filling. A rubber ball is actually better than a tennis ball because it weighs a bit more, behaving like a hard ball in flight, but it won't hurt if it hits you. I frequently use a rubber ball when I have outfield practice, especially for young players who are having trouble catching. Go to a hard ball for short catches when you can.

Remember, a key to confidence is not pushing too hard. If it's not working, don't get angry. Start from a position that allows the player to do well, and gradually increase the difficulty. Recognize and celebrate improvement! If you start with too difficult a distance, the child will only learn to fail. If it's not working, make it easier. A challenge is OK, but an impossible challenge is only a negative experience.

## Catching Fly Balls

Catching fly balls is not that difficult, but it is one of the last things kids learn to do well. The main idea in catching pop-ups is to get under the ball so it's traveling right at the head. I know this sounds strange, but it's the best way to catch. It's just like hitting: You must keep your eye on the ball, and you can see it best when it's coming right at your eyes. The glove should be above the head when catching the ball, fingers up, palm outward.

Many kids are afraid to try this for obvious reasons, especially if they have already been hit by a ball. So they let the ball fall to one side of them and try to catch it at the waist. The trouble with such a catch is they have to calculate two more angles, and it's much easier to misjudge it. (See figure 3-1.) If the ball is coming right at the eye, all the player has to do is stick her glove in the way at the right time. Now, this is why I use rubber or tennis balls for younger kids. They know it won't hurt since it's rubber, so they will try

FIGURE 3-1
## CATCHING POP-UPS

Proper position—directly under the ball, glove high, palm outward, two hands.

Improper position—allowing ball to drop into lowered glove. It is much tougher to catch.

harder to get under it. Take it slow, start with a short distance if you need to, and, over a few weeks, work out to a longer distance. Pick an appropriate angle so the sun is not in their eyes. Build confidence slowly. It may take a very long time, so just relax and be patient.

Kids usually misjudge fly balls by coming in too far and letting the ball go over their heads. So when your child shows that he can catch the ball, start to vary the distance. First throw over his head. Then throw one short, then to the right or left. On line drives to the right of the fielder, he will have to turn his glove backward and catch it backhanded. On throws over his head, tell him to *turn and run*, not just backpedal! (See figure 3-2.) He will get to the ball faster and can make a more relaxed catch.

As noted earlier, if the ball goes directly to the fielder, she must catch the ball above her head, two hands out, with her fingers up and palm facing the sky. Remind her to try to catch the ball in the webbing of the glove, between the thumb and index finger. This

FIGURE 3-2

## CHASING DOWN POP-UPS

Backhanding a ball hit to side opposite glove.

On deep fly balls, do not backpedal. Turn and run back to get under it.

reduces the chance that the ball will pop out, and it avoids stinging the palm of the hand. Also, tell the fielder to use both hands. The free hand stays by the glove and smothers the ball when it hits the glove. This accomplishes two things: It keeps the ball from popping out of the glove, and it gets the ball into the throwing hand faster so the fielder wastes no time getting the ball back to the infield.

Fungo practice, as it is called, involves a coach hitting the ball to the fielders, either infield or outfield. It takes some skill to do. That is why fungo bats are extra big. For young players, I find it more effective to throw the ball. You may too! Don't throw your arm out. Always warm up first with a dozen or so short throws, then go for some longer ones. Just get a dozen or so long ones in and that is all each player will need at each session. After a while, use the bat.

It's good to move to different drills, just a few minutes on each. Variety keeps everyone more interested. Focus on different skills each day.

It may be that a child will miss nearly every catch at first. "No problem," tell him. "Tomorrow or the next day we'll catch one or two. Then after that more." Focus on slight improvement. Don't set expectations too high. Don't get frustrated—your player will sense your frustration and feel it too. After a while, he will improve.

## Catching Grounders

I think catching infield grounders is the toughest thing in youth baseball. It takes a keen, quick reflex, speed and good concentration to be an infielder. Again, some people figure that you either have it or you don't.

OK, so everybody can't play everywhere, no problem. Eye-hand coordination varies for kids. It can be tested. Chapter eight discusses how to improve vision and coordination. In any event, give each kid a shot at it. Coaches tend to quickly pick the best infielder early, and the other kids don't see a grounder for the rest of the season. Don't let this happen at young ages.

The first thing is to find a smooth surface. Most grass fields are terrible. They only teach a kid to fear grounders since bad hops occur very frequently. A dirt field is much better, and you can rake out any ruts and remove stones. I often took my son to a parking lot. City parents can use a side street if traffic is very light. Throw the ball sidearm, or somehow make sure you release it about two feet from the ground—the height where a bat would hit it. At first let him stand fairly close, and throw the ball softly, getting it to him on one bounce. Again, throwing the ball works as well as hitting it and takes less skill on your part. Also, you can put the ball exactly where you want it. After a while, when he can handle it, make it tougher. Give a couple of bounces, vary the speed, throw to the right or left. As in the outfield, the fielder reverses the glove position on shots to the side opposite the glove hand, catching it backhanded. After skills are improved, move onto a regular infield and use a bat.

As with outfielding, the idea is to get in front of the ball so it's coming right at you. Catch the ball to the side only if you must to reach it. The player initially stands in a crouch, facing the batter, legs spread out a bit, knees and hips bent, hands and gloves down by the knees, weight forward on the toes so the fielder can spring either way. Many infielders get themselves moving a bit toward the batter with the pitch, so the muscles are in motion, ready to spring. (See figure 3-3.) When the ball is hit, the player *springs*, not steps, to get quickly to the spot where she can make the play.

I used to tell my players that infielders have to "stand up and sit down at the same time." The legs are spread apart, left foot up, right foot back. The knees are bent so the backside is down low. (Not really sitting of course, but it makes the point. We want the body low.) Most players prefer to bend over at the waist; a waist bend is needed but not at the expense of bending the knees. The back and head should be down, back nearly parallel to the ground, head on the ball. "Bend from the knee, not from the waist." Repeat this sentence constantly. (See figure 3-3.)

A critical element of good fielding in any position is to use both hands. In the old days gloves were so small that two hands were essential. Now, with larger gloves kids get bad habits. I recommend smaller gloves for infielders. A good drill is to tape the hand onto the outside of the glove. Use masking tape. This limits the fielder's control of the glove and forces the use of two hands.

Finally, the glove should be down, way down. "Come up with some dirt on it," I always say. Honus Wagner used to throw a handful of dirt with the ball. If the ball goes under the glove, it's all over. Start the glove low, and bring it forward and up to meet the ball. Visualize a triangle with the glove and both feet. Players often expect the ball to bounce up to them, but sometimes it doesn't. If it was hit on the top of the ball, the topspin will make it skim the ground. The glove must always be low in anticipation of this. If the ball skims, it's easier to bring the glove up to meet it than down.

Another popular tip is to tell your infielders to visualize a funnel with the open mouth receiving the ball and channeling or funneling it up to the waist. A key here is that the hands must be soft, giving way to the ball. The scooping action brings the glove forward to the ball, then gently back to the waist. Tell them to think of their hands as soft.

Tell fielders that it's important not to stand back on the heels, just waiting for the ball to play you. A fielder must play the ball. If the ball is slow, run in to get it; otherwise get in front and scoop it up. The forward action is the aggressiveness needed to command

FIGURE 3-3

# FIELDING GROUNDERS

Proper stance as ball is pitched. Body
low, knees bent, waist bent, balanced,
glove down and out, head up, poised.

Stand up and sit down: Get low, bend
knees and lower glove.

Keep head down and scoop the ball up
and back to the waist.

the ball. Again, if you practice on a smooth surface, these skills will
be much easier to demonstrate and learn.

The biggest problems with kids catching grounders are (1) not
getting in front of the ball; (2) using only one hand; (3) not getting
the glove low enough (not bending the knees enough); and (4)
coming up too soon, especially with the head.

I had an all-star first baseman in 1987, a ten-year-old named Chris.
He could hit the ball a mile, but his fielding was not consistent.

One day before regular practice, he and his father got there early to practice grounders. He had made some errors the previous game, and I was worried a bit. I guess they were too! I watched him closely, focusing on different parts of his body. After several plays I saw it! Just as the ball was about to be caught, he would lift his head up, and then up would follow his shoulders, his arms and, of course, his glove. It's understandable. Kids are worried about the ball getting a bad hop into the face, so they lift or turn their heads. I told Chris about it, and then kept saying, "stay down, stay down, stay calm" as the ball approached him. It took a while, but he started to adjust. If he keeps working at it, he will eliminate the problem permanently.

Reflexes are important in infield play. So you practice them. I used to get two balls and stand about 20 feet from my son. I would throw one, then throw the other one just as he was releasing the first ball back to me. Quick, to the left, to the right, change speeds. Quick. It improves the reflexes. That is another drill you can do for a few minutes.

Remember, as with hitting, don't be impatient with the misses, the booted balls, the errors. They happen even to the pros. Reward the catches with a smile, or "way to go." And repeat, repeat, repeat! Repetition is the backbone of success and improvement. The more the better.

Make it fun. A fun drill is the Goalie Grounder. Put up two empty bottles a short distance to the left and right, like a soccer goal, and see how many grounders he can stop. Keep score, have a goal. Increase it over time. Tell him constantly to keep his eye on the ball. (See figure 3-4.)

## THE GLOVE

The glove may be the most important thing about catching. Each child needs a decent glove, and it must be broken in. It is nearly impossible to catch a ball with the cheap, rigid, plastic junk you find in a toy store. The ball will just jump out every time. Even a good glove takes a year to break in, soften up.

When I get a new glove, I literally beat it up. Rub glove oil into it, and bend every inch of it back and forth. Keep bending the fingers back and forth, hit it with a bat, jump on it. Years ago players

FIGURE 3-4
## GOALIE GROUNDER DRILL

Set up cones as goalposts on sand or soft grass and have fielder try to stop grounders.

used to drop a new glove in a pail of water and hang it out to dry (I've never tried it). The point is that the glove should be soft enough to collapse on the ball. I've seen so many kids get a negative picture of their ability because of the cheap junk gloves they got.

When practice is over, leave a ball in the pocket of the glove and wrap the glove around it. In the off-season, wrap tape around the glove to keep the ball in place.

## THROWING

There is really not a whole lot I can tell you about throwing. Pitching yes, throwing no. But there is a lot you can do about it. Throwing is almost totally dependent on just doing it. Each player needs to throw a ball a few thousand times before he or she gets the smooth style of a decent throw. So suggest to parents that they regularly have a catch with their son or daughter. It's something you can do anywhere, anytime. Having a catch is not only a great American pastime, at early ages it is critical for developing a good throw.

Start nice and easy, 15 to 25 feet apart, and slowly move back to 60 feet. The more times your child throws the ball, the faster and better her arm will work out the coordination needed. It will come.

## Throwing Basics

Of course, there are a few basics you can look for. One year I had a young girl named Suzanne on my team. She was a good athlete, but she had never seen a baseball. Everybody throws awkwardly when they are just starting—as I said, it takes a thousand or so tosses to begin developing a smooth throw.

Anyway, I looked at Suzanne carefully. And, I repeat, to be a coaching parent you must force yourself to focus on different parts of the body, to find things the player is doing wrong. I looked at her foot position and saw that she was throwing off her left foot; that is, she was pushing off her left foot and stepping forward with her right foot—it was backwards! The idea in throwing (for righties) is to step with the left and push off on the right foot as you begin the throw, landing on the left as you release the throw. (See figure 3-5.) When the fielder is ready to throw, she should stand a bit sideways, point the left shoulder at the target, reach back with the ball, then step and drive. I also tell my players always to get set before they throw, plant the back foot, and get off a good throw.

Sometimes there is no time to get set, and a fielder has to throw off balance or on the run. That's when many throwing errors are made.

Another tip about throwing is to reach back with the ball and then after you cock the arm and wrist to throw, extend the arm. Many kids are arm-throwers. They bend their elbow too much and throw entirely with their arm—it looks like they are literally "throwing the arm" instead of the ball. When the arm is extended, the shoulder becomes the fulcrum and brings the strength of the entire body into the throw. The hands and arm move in a circular motion. The elbow-bent arm-thrower cuts off the power coming from the right leg, right hip and right shoulder. He gets less power on the throw, and his arm will quickly tire since it is doing all the work. Remember to keep the elbow high—at or over the shoulder.

FIGURE 3-5
## THROWING FORM

Proper form. Pushing off same foot as throwing arm (right arm, right foot). NOTE: Left shoulder originally was pointed toward target, full arm extension, left foot steps toward target.

## Grip

Grip on the ball is very standard—thumb on bottom, the next two fingers (index and middle) on top, the last two fingers tucked on the side. If the player's hand is small, let her use the three middle fingers on top, with only the pinky tucked on the side. Fingers can straddle or cross the seams, but in a fielding play she won't have time to worry about seams. Also, make sure the ball is not set back in the hand too far—there should be some space between the palm and the ball. The idea is to throw with the fingers. (See figure 3-6.)

## Aim

Never use this word! Aim comes from the body. You *throw to* a player. The left (nonthrowing) shoulder and the left foot both point in the direction of the target. Eyes must look right at the target. Some kids like to throw the ball high in a big soft arc. I think it's

FIGURE 3-6
## GRIPPING THE BALL

Proper grip. Ball not set too deeply into hand.

If the hand is small, all three middle fingers may be placed on top.

because they feel they control it better, maybe it's because it's easier. Anyway, a throw should always be as hard and level as possible, a line drive. A ball thrown straight on a line is called a "rope." This means it was thrown straight, like a rope clothesline. I always tell my players to throw right at the other kid's chest or head. That is the best height to catch the ball, so that's where the thrower should throw it.

For infielders, as I noted earlier, the key is to get the ball out of the glove as quickly as possible. The throwing hand should go for the ball the moment it hits the glove and make the transition very quickly.

## Velocity

The velocity of the throw depends on where the fielder is playing. A third baseman or shortstop really has to rifle the ball to get it to first base. However, the second baseman needs only to ensure a firm throw to first base. If he throws too hard, he risks a control problem, throwing the ball away, and it's much harder for the first baseman to catch. This also applies to the pitcher throwing to first.

The shortstop will make a softer throw to second base on a ball hit to his left side with a runner on first. Field the ball, turn to the bag, and just lob the ball, underhanded if he is very close to the second baseman. This also happens on grounders to the first baseman. The second baseman softly lobs the ball to the pitcher covering first base, if necessary. Run to the base if it's not a close play, but throw to the pitcher as a rule.

An outfielder, on the other hand, always throws hard. The key to her throw is to get rid of the ball quickly. How many times do we see the outfielders stand there holding the ball while runners are flying around the bases?

Of course, the problem with such an outfielder is that he doesn't know where to throw the ball. He has to think about it, look at the runners, decide where to throw. He sees a lot of commotion in the infield, he is excited because he just caught the ball, and he doesn't know what to do. So the runners run, and the parents scream, and the poor kid gets so nervous he throws the ball into the parking lot.

## THE CUTOFF AND THROWING AHEAD
## OF THE LEAD RUNNER

Outfielders are always supposed to hit the cutoff. With no one on, if the ball is hit to left field or to the left of center field, the shortstop is usually the cutoff. If it's to the right side, the second baseman usually gets it. (See figure 3-7.) With runners on base, the cutoff concept becomes a bit more complicated.

Since this book is for youth coaches and parents, you may wonder whether I really need to go into detail on the difficult concept of the cutoff. It is certainly a tough concept to master and takes much precious practice time. With young kids we are pressed just to get them to be able to hit and catch, let alone deal with difficult cutoff concepts. I rarely see teams do much in this area. Much of the problem about the usual cutoff responsibility of the shortstop and second baseman is that many coaches don't know the underlying concepts. Some just say, "Always throw the ball to second base." Well, I agree that it's better than nothing, better than holding the ball. But it's not baseball. It's not defense. And a coach who doesn't understand the concept obviously can't teach it.

FIGURE 3-7

## CUTOFF PLAY WITH BASES EMPTY

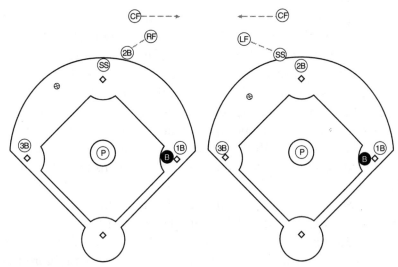

Ball hit to right side. Second baseman stands 15 feet off bag if shallow hit, and moves out toward outfielder if further relay is needed. Shortstop covers the bag.

Ball hit to left side. Shortstop stands 15 feet off if shallow hit, and moves out toward outfielder if further relay is needed. Second baseman covers bag.

Actually, it's really very logical, commonsense stuff. I recommend you learn it and then talk about the concepts. It may take a whole season to get the kids to get the hang of it, but it's part of the game, and it will save runs on defense. My suggestion would be to spend some time on the concept at very young ages, but don't go crazy trying to get the kids to master it unless you practice every day. Just tell them that they need to understand it, and will be expected to learn it over time. In the meantime be satisfied if they get the ball to second base. By the time they're ten to eleven years old you can start pushing it.

The concept of the cutoff is based on the need to *stop the lead runner*. The lead runner is the one who is closest to scoring. If there are runners on first and second bases, the one on second is the lead runner. If the only runner is on first, then that is the lead runner—the runner you want to stop. The way to stop the lead runner is to throw to the base ahead of him. Perhaps the most important defensive concept is to *throw ahead of the lead runner.* It's very simple—you just have to know where the lead runner is and throw toward the base in front of him.

So, on a single to the outfield, a lead runner on first will get to second easily. The objective is to stop him from going to third base, so that's where to throw the ball—toward third base. Since the runner will be on second base by the time the outfielder gets the ball, the base ahead of the runner is third base. If the outfielder throws to second base, a quick runner can go to third by the time the second baseman catches the ball and throws to third.

If the play starts with the lead runner on second, he will go to third easily on a single to the outfield. That means the base ahead of the lead runner is home plate, so that's the direction of the throw! If you want to stop runs, you must get the ball in front of the runner, especially when he is headed home. The idea of throwing in front of the lead runner will help to make it clearer. Just tell the players to first consider who the lead runner is, then they can figure that the throw on a ground ball to outfield must be to two bases in front of that runner.

If there is a runner on third, forget about him on a hit to the outfield. On a ball hit safely to the outfield, a runner on third will always score, so he is never the lead runner. Outfielders only worry about a runner on first or second. The only time a runner on third comes into the picture is on a fly ball, when the runner will tag up and try to go home.

The real complexity comes in when the lead runner is not the only person on base. You also want to stop the batter from going to second base, if possible. If the outfielder throws all the way to third base or home, the batter will probably have time to advance. So to get in position to have a play on *both* the lead runner and the batter, position a fielder called a *cutoff* in the path of the ball. If the lead runner was on first, the cutoff stands in the path of the throw from outfield, about twenty feet or so before third base. This cutoff fielder has the option of letting the ball go on to third base if needed to get the lead runner, or cutting it off to hold or make a play on the batter. He may, for instance, feel that there is a better chance to get the batter out if he is running to second base. Or, if the ball is thrown off-line and will not get to the third baseman, then the

FIGURE 3-8

## CUTOFF PLAY WITH LEAD RUNNER ON FIRST

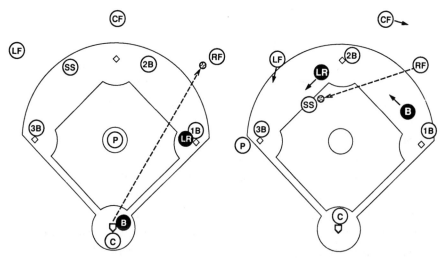

Start of play. Ball hit to right field. Lead runner (LR) on first.

Proper position. Right fielder throws toward third base in front of lead runner. Shortstop is cutoff to hold batter at first. Pitcher backs up third base by 15 feet.

ball should automatically be cut off. In this instance the cutoff is just trying to keep control of the ball, and not let a bad throw go into foul territory.

So the cutoff player needs to line up between the outfielder and third base. With a runner on first, I like the shortstop to be the cutoff. (See figure 3-8.) The second baseman is needed to hold the runner on the base. If the ball is coming from right field, the shortstop can best decide whether to let the ball go through to the third baseman or to cut it off. If the lead runner stopped at second, the shortstop will cut it off anyway. If the shortstop judges that the runner will clearly make it to third (and here the third baseman must yell to her what to do), she cuts it off to keep the player who hit the ball from going to second base.

Read this a few times. Once you have the concept in mind, you will automatically know what to do. The general concept that you must etch onto the fielders' minds is to throw toward the base in front of the lead runner. The coach must designate a fielder who should be ready to cut off that throw to hold the batter or another runner from advancing.

Using a cutoff is not a matter of memorizing what to do, it's a principle that says simply stop the lead runner by throwing ahead of him, and give yourself a shot at other runners by hitting the cutoff. The team chatters to each other, with the coach's help, about who the lead runner is, who the cutoff is, and what base the outfielder must throw to. This chatter goes on incessantly before each pitch.

Suppose the lead runner is on second. The goal is to stop her from going home on a single. So the outfielder throws ahead of the lead runner—he throws home. The chatter should reach a fever pitch here, since a runner is in scoring position. The whole team needs to understand that this runner is a threat. For this play the cutoff is the pitcher. (See figure 3-9.) The pitcher is the closest player to home. If there is a play at the plate, the pitcher first looks at the ball to see if it was thrown straight. If not, she will probably have to cut it off, since they will not get the runner at the plate anyway, and she needs to make sure the other runners don't advance.

Now, I know I'll catch some flak here, because in big league play the pitcher always backs up home when there is a possible play at the plate, and, depending on which side the ball was hit to, the third baseman or the first baseman is the cutoff. Actually, at advanced levels of play, there are many scenarios for cutoff and backing up, depending on the number of runners and the depth of the hit. At high school and college levels, the kids play every day, and have time to practice these plays. At young ages you need to keep it a bit simpler. At the youngest ages, just getting it in to second base may be the best you can accomplish. I believe coaches need to get what they can, and then push a bit further.

After the first edition of this book came out, I got a call from a coach in Seattle who had an assistant coach arguing with him about my cutoff locations. The assistant had played college ball, and felt that the big league cutoff responsibilities should be taught. Well, my response was that the kids weren't playing on a big league field. A Little League field is smaller, has a closer backstop, and involves a shorter throw from outfield, particularly on grounders. Therefore, the cutoff game should be tailored to the field at hand, and to what

FIGURE 3-9

## CUTOFF PLAY WITH LEAD RUNNER ON SECOND

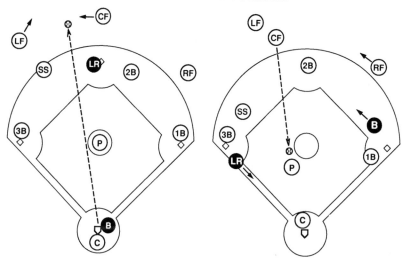

Start of play. Ball hit to center field. LR on second base.

Proper position. Center fielder throws ahead of lead runner threatening toward home. Pitcher is cutoff to hold batter at first.

the kids can grasp. I like the pitcher in the middle on a play at the plate. (See figure 3-9.) When the kids move up to bigger fields, the pitcher goes behind the catcher with a lead runner on second. On most Little League fields, the backstop does the job, and the pitcher is more useful as a cutoff on a throw home. If the pitcher lets the ball go through to the plate, he should then turn and run toward the plate in case the ball gets by the catcher.

If you teach the pitcher to back up home and want the first or third baseman to be cutoff on a play at the plate, that's fine! I taught it when my kids moved to 90-foot bases. I just found that my way worked better and was simpler for young players.

Now, if there is no one on base at all then the batter is the lead runner. Then the throw goes to second base, ahead of the batter, the lead runner. So the adage we always hear at Little League games about throwing to second base is only correct when there is no one on base. Here, as noted earlier, the cutoff is the shortstop or second baseman, depending on where the ball was hit. In Little League play the distance is so short that the outfielders are often very close to second base when they field the ball. A cutoff only goes out to the fielder when it is needed. It depends on the distance and the strength of the fielder's throw.

Nothing is automatic, which is why it's best for kids to learn the concepts behind what they need to do. Then they can figure out what to do in a given play. I adjust things based on the abilities of fielders. Again, field chatter is the best way to get these ideas to sink in. Constantly remind players who the lead runners are.

So there it is—that's what the cutoff is about. It's logical and really very simple when you think about it. The purpose of defense is to stop runs from being scored. The outfielders therefore try to get the ball in front of the lead runner. They direct the ball to the next base to which this lead runner would go. If there is a chance to get that runner out, the ball is allowed to go through. If there is no play, the cutoff fielder catches the ball to see if he can make a play on the other runners, to stop them from advancing. The more you go over the concept, the simpler it will become to your team.

Of course, when the ball goes past the outfielder, to the fence, the strategy is the same, but the second baseman or shortstop has to go out farther to get the relay. Children can't throw the ball to the plate from 200 feet away. So the shortstop or second baseman goes out to get the relay who then turns to see if there is a play. The other mid-infielder can help by yelling to the cutoff and pointing where to throw the ball. On a ball hit to the fence, anyone on second or third base will score. The only hope is to stop the runner on first (if there was one) from going home or to catch the batter going to second base (if he is slow) or to third base. (See figure 3-10.) Since these are the only plays possible, you focus on them and ignore the rest. So, the cutoff takes the throw from the deep outfielder and wheels to go home if directed to do so. Otherwise, he looks to third.

## RUNDOWNS

Often a runner is caught between two bases. This situation calls for a rundown. It's a simple play that is usually fouled up. Its elements are as follows.

FIGURE 3-10

## CUTOFF PLAY ON DEEP HIT TO THE FENCE

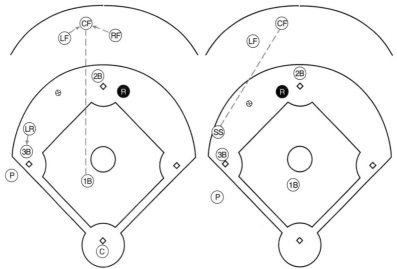

A runner on first (LR) at the start of the play will likely reach third base easily, so the outfielder or relay (2B if needed) should throw toward home, to the cutoff (first baseman). Pitcher backs up third base.

With no one on, the batter (B) will likely reach second base, so throw toward third base, to the cutoff (shortstop). Pitcher backs up third base.

1. Get the runner to fully commit himself. Whoever has the ball, usually an infielder, must understand that the runner will want to see where the ball is thrown and then run in the opposite direction. Therefore, the fielder, if this happens, should charge at the runner and get him to commit first.

2. If the runner tries to advance to the next base, get the ball quickly to that base. You always want to run the runner back to the prior base and attempt the putout there. That way, if the putout fails, at least the runner will not have advanced. This is particularly important, for obvious reasons, when the rundown is between third base and home plate.

3. The fielder with the ball should hold it high, feigning a throw while running hard on the inside of the base path. This will confuse the runner who is trying to anticipate the throw. A good faked throw may get the runner to stop, to change direction, allowing the fielder

to tag her. A well-executed rundown should require only one throw to retire the runner.

4. The rest is "feel"—if the fielder can make the tag she does so, otherwise she throws to the base in time for that fielder to take the tag.

5. The fielder covering the base toward which the runner is heading should be off the base at least several feet toward the runner on the inside of the base path. Then if the throw is a bit late she still has time to make a tag. How many times do we see a runner slide under a late throw to a fielder standing on the bag? If you see a rundown in the pros, the receiving fielder is usually off the bag and calls for the throw when the runner is close. Note: All fielders should play slightly to the inside of the base path to avoid hitting the runner with the ball.

6. Other available fielders who are not guarding another runner should back up the fielder involved in the rundown. They are often needed.

## CONCLUSION

So that is what a coach or parent needs to know generally about fielding. In fact, given the amount of time you have for practice, it's probably more than you can get done. The main things are to go and have a catch, use a rubber ball for outfield practice, throw the ball instead of batting it, urge kids to get under a pop-up and down low and in front of the grounders. Talk about defensive dynamics and the need to hit the cutoff while throwing in front of the lead runner. Every kid will improve, especially if you spend the time. Remember, parents, a few minutes every other day is not much, but it can accomplish a great deal. Try it! It may come slowly for both of you, so be patient and enjoy the improvement as it comes.

# Chapter Four

# RUNNING AND SLIDING

One great thing about baseball is that the part that is the most fun—hitting—is also the easiest to teach. Running, however, particularly speed in running, is like fielding: If you don't have it naturally, you can improve it only with a great deal of practice. I repeat, the adage that you can't make a kid a fielder or a pitcher or a runner is not true. But it does take longer, and the key is just doing a lot of it. Also, if kids don't get sufficient leg exercise they can get slower; I've seen it happen.

Usually kids who are slow play third base, first base or catcher, since they don't need as much speed or range at those positions. They do need quickness and good reflexes; they just don't need speed.

However, speed in the outfield and quickness in the infield do win games. Speed on the base path will score more runs. So a fast kid will get more playing time.

For young kids you can increase speed somewhat by running wind sprints. A good workout is a half dozen thirty-yard dashes. Sprints give additional leg strength to get up to speed more quickly. Acceleration comes from leg strength. Proper running form is on the balls of the toes, head and shoulders forward, arms churning up and down.

Running up stairs or hills is good for quickness. There is a difference between quickness and speed. Quickness is mobility in a short distance. A child can improve quickness more easily than speed. See the speed and agility drills in chapter six.

As noted earlier, defensive players always need to be on their toes, weight forward, body hunched forward and down to lower the center of gravity. Keeping the weight on the toes also allows the infielder to dance, spring and hop as needed to field the ball and quickly switch to a throwing stance.

## RUNNING BASES

Base runners have to do the same thing—weight down and forward, on the toes, on the balls of the feet, ready to spring. A player running to a base, especially first base, should always run as fast as possible. How many times have you seen a player out at first base because he turned to see where the ball was or slowed just before he got to the base? The runner should just put his head down and run like there's no tomorrow.

When a runner runs to first base on an infield hit, the process begins in the batter's box. Many hits are lost when a kid gets a slow start out of the box. Once contact is made, the batter must not worry about where the ball is; her first instinct must be to run, to explode from the box. A righty batter will push off with the left foot, taking a small step with the right, lower the body, and start pumping the arms. She runs hard and through the bag. Don't hop onto it, run through it. A player may overrun first base by as much as needed to slow down. Some people erroneously think that a runner can't turn toward second base. There is no rule on which way to turn, and the runner can safely return to first as long as she did not make a move that appears to be an attempt to go to second base. It's a good practice, however, to turn away from the field.

If the ball was hit to the outfield the runner should run a hook pattern toward first base. (See figure 4-1.) This means that the runner makes an arc, about 6 to 8 feet into foul territory on a Little League size field. Start to make the arc about halfway or more to first base. The arc helps to set the runner on a more direct course to second base, if he chooses to go.

When a runner is going to pass a base, she plants her left foot on the inside corner of the bag and leans into the turn. This can save much time, a step or two. (See figure 4-1.) The base can be touched with either foot, so don't get jumbled up. The left foot, however, is preferable.

Once the runner gets to a base he has to look at the ball and decide whether to advance. Runners should always know where the ball is, and watch or anticipate where and how hard it will be thrown. They must also listen to the base coach, but, since base coaches are often a kid who is not playing, they need to rely on their own judgment too. I like my runners to lull the outfielders by

FIGURE 4-1
## RUNNING BASES

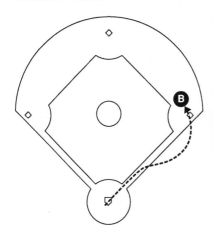

Hook pattern rounding first base.

Plant foot on inside corner and lean in.

pretending they are going to stop (if the outfielder is preparing to throw), but get as much ground as they can. Then if the throw is not good, or if it's not to the base in front of them, they can sprint to that base. A runner who hits the ball to the outfield should go about a fourth to a third of the way to second base, and then see if the throw is other than to the bag in front of him—if not, he goes. Many kids can make the remaining 40 feet before someone can catch the throw and relay it to the second baseman. After some practice a child will know what he or she can do.

In chapter three I talked a bit about throwing in front of the lead runner. Well, the offensive side of this is that the lead runner should look for chances to advance an extra base, especially if the ball isn't thrown ahead of her. Runners should always make things happen, take a wide turn at a base, not so wide that they can't get back safely, but wide enough to draw a throw. If the throw is bad, they go. Some boys and girls are so fast that they automatically go when the ball is thrown behind them, because they know they will beat the next relay.

## SIGNALS AND BASE COACHING

For me, one of the joys of managing a youth team was coaching third base. Most rules allow one coach on the baselines, and I always took advantage of it. Out on the field is where the action is, and I always wanted to be close to it. Third base was my spot. Coaches are more useful at third since the decision to send a runner home is such an important one.

As noted earlier, the main strategy at youth ages, particularly for kids under twelve years old, is to keep the kids running. Take risks—they usually pay off. It takes a good throw, a good catch and a good tag to get a runner out, and three out of three is more the exception than the rule at young ages.

When a runner approaches third, he must do one of four things: (1) run to the bag and stay on it, (2) slide into it, (3) take a turn for a few steps toward home to draw a throw or to be ready to sprint home if an opportunity arises, or (4) run through the base and sprint home. The sign for the first option is both hands up overhead, signaling, "No need to slide. The ball is not close, but stay on the bag." The signal to slide is both hands down, palms down. When it's real close I lie right down on the ground to signal that a low, low slide is needed. I point to the side of the bag he should slide toward, usually the inside. The runner should then look, not at the ball, but at the location of the fielder's glove to see how to avoid the tag. The signal to take a wide turn is to point to the spot on the ground the player should run to. Pick a spot 5 to 10 feet past the base. The runner and the coach then look toward the ball to see if any possibility arises to run home. The runner must stay close enough to the bag to dart back if the defense makes a play on him. If the coach wants to send the runner home, he windmills his extended left arm clockwise. I used to run a few steps with the runner to encourage him to dig hard and slide low at the plate.

With a runner on third and less than two out, I repeatedly warn the player to stand on the bag if the ball is hit to the outfield. This is so she can tag up and score. I'd tell her to not look at the ball but just listen for my go signal.

Not all coaches use signals for the batter and runners on the pitch. This is because there are few bunts and also because most steals are on passed balls. However, signals are part of baseball. They are useful at all levels, and kids need to learn the concepts.

Signals are basically a series of hand movements touching the coach's body, such as touching the beak of the hat, the mouth, the chest, a shoulder, the elbow, clapping hands. A typical scenario might be: touch the cap beak = a steal, touch the chin = take a pitch (don't swing), touch the chest = bunt, touch a shoulder = hit and run. Other signals can be used to call for a fake bunt, a hit to the right side of the infield, a swing at the first pitch and a sacrifice.

The way to stop the other teams from stealing your signs is to have a "key" sign that signals that the *next* sign is the one to follow. For example, a key sign might be touching the top of the head. So, using the above signs, a steal would be signaled by (1) a series of dummy signs, (2) touch the top of the head, (3) touch the beak of the cap, and then (4) finish with a few other dummy signs. Once the batter or runners (all of whom must be watching your signs) see you touch the top of your head, they know the next sign is the real one.

## STEALING BASES

Stealing bases is the worst part of Little League ball. The distance between bases is very short, and the rule against taking a lead makes it very, very hard to steal except on a passed ball. However, there are so many passed balls and wild pitches that runners pretty much advance at will. Occasionally you get a decent catcher who will hold it down, but stealing on passed balls dominates the game. I don't like it, but that's the way it is. So I keep my players running. When they are on third base, I tell them to nonchalantly move toward the catcher after the ball passes the batter, and if they advance ten feet, to steal as soon as the catcher throws back to the pitcher. If the pitcher is on the mound, the play will work. I can't say I like it. It's just not baseball to have so many runs scored on steals. Some leagues prohibit stealing, or at least stealing home. I agree with that—make them hit the ball. But until they change the rules, I will keep the kids running.

There are times to steal and times to hold. The best time to steal is with two outs and the only runner on first. He needs to get into scoring position, particularly in a close game. The worst time to steal is when the other team has a large lead. Outs are valuable when you are behind, and it's not good to waste one on a marginal steal. When you have a big lead, it's poor form to rub it in, but I've

FIGURE 4-2
## RUNNING POSITION

Ready to run, low, can move quickly in either direction.

learned that no lead is large enough in youth baseball. I've held kids up with a ten-run lead and gone on to lose by one run. You can be darned if you do and darned if you don't! If the catcher is sloppy about throws to the pitcher, have your base coaches keep the kids ready to run, especially runners at second or third. If the catcher has a poor arm, keep 'em running all day!

When you talk about running, talk about the need to lower the center of gravity, stay on the toes, look for chances to run, and run hard when you go. Make a list of the basics and yell them out every so often. Repetition works. (See figure 4-2.)

## SLIDING

Sliding is an important part of baserunning. Many outs or successful steals are based on how good the slide is. I know that very few coaches teach it. It may be that the ground is too hard, or the coach doesn't feel he has time. But there are basics to sliding, and it can be practiced.

I have kids practice sliding by getting a large piece of cardboard, like a refrigerator box, and laying it on the ground. The kids take off their shoes and run and slide on the cardboard. Remove any staples! It works and they love it.

FIGURE 4-3

**SLIDING**

Throw the left foot toward the base, bend the right leg for a cushion, hands off the ground, slide low, avoid the tag.

The technique to sliding is demonstrated in figure 4-3. The right leg is bent and tucked in under the left, and the slide is pretty much flat on the butt. A lot of people turn on the slide, but that hurts more and raises the body surface. The key to sliding is to keep every part of the body low to the ground. So the best slide is one where the player is virtually lying down on her back at the time of contact. Players should avoid breaking the fall with their hands; it's very easy to sprain a wrist. Besides, the backside gives enough cushion. Keep the hands up, off the ground, but not so high that they can be tagged.

The player should slide away from the ball. On a throw from the outfield, slide inside the base (second base). For a play at the plate, slide to the umpire side of home plate, away from the throw. This is called a *hook slide*.

Some gung ho players slide head first, diving at the base. It does get you there a bit more quickly, but it's very dangerous. I've seen sprained wrists and bloody noses, even a broken back. Of course, at twelve years old or younger these kids don't need to dive. If it happens I caution the player against it. It's not worth the risk.

# Chapter Five

# BASEBALL POSITIONS

At young ages kids should play various, if not all, positions. They certainly should practice at different positions. Early in the season I have every boy or girl on the team pitch during practice. During defensive drills they play every position. I do this because it's good for them, and it helps me to see what their skills are and who is best for the more important positions up the middle—shortstop, second base, center field. The earlier chapters of this book identified some basics for all positions, and you should try to spend some time on each area. Emphasize hitting, but work also on fielding, throwing and running.

This chapter addresses each individual position. It will help you get a better understanding of defensive concepts from the perspective of the individual position. This will add to your overview of the game and put you in a better position to decide what position a player should play. If you are a parent, you can advise your child what position he or she may be best suited for.

## CATCHER

No one can pick up a team like a catcher. Catchers face their team most of the time and so are in the best position to encourage fellow players, keep them on their toes. A catcher should be a leader, an aggressive kid. He can really inspire the team from his vantage point.

It takes a special kind of kid to hang in at this position. It's tough to get kids interested in it and even tougher to find a good one. If you want to guarantee that your child plays a lot in each game, tell her to be a catcher. She'll play all she wants at that position.

Catchers are usually very tough-minded kids. They have to be able to take some pain. The ball often strains the thumb in the catching hand. Catchers get bruised by the ball and run over by runners. It's dirty and hot underneath all of the equipment. They get up and down on every pitch and must be into the game more

FIGURE 5-1

## CATCHING POSITION

Great stance. Low crouch. Weight forward on balls of toes. Right foot back a bit. Upper leg parallel to ground. Good target. Free hand behind back.

than anyone on the field. I love catchers! They are the closest thing to old-time baseball, a gutsy down-and-dirty game.

As noted earlier, catching is good for a big kid (or any size) who has no speed or cannot really play well defensively. There is a defensive position for everybody—if a player can hit you must find a position she can play.

Catchers must get used to the crouch, on the toes of both feet. If she is a righty, the right foot is back a bit. Weight should be forward on the balls of the feet, heels lightly touching the ground. Putting one knee down on the ground is no good. That reduces mobility and agility, and it increases the risk of injury. The upper leg is parallel to the ground and the waist is bent forward. (See figure 5-1.)

Little League catchers often get too far back behind the plate. Obviously, they worry about getting hit with the bat. They don't realize that the batter is stepping forward, his body moving toward the pitcher, and there is really no way the bat will hit them. They must get close to the batters, because that is where the strike zone is. If they move back too far, then the pitcher has to throw higher to reach the glove. Also, the strike zone shrinks to the umpire's perspective as he moves back from the batter. Tell the catcher to set up so his glove is just an inch or two behind the batter's hands or elbow, whichever is his backmost point.

The catcher has to let the ball come to the glove, and catch it in the pocket. If she reaches out for it, there is a chance the bat will nick the glove. This doesn't happen often, but the batter gets a free trip to first base when it does. Pitches above the waist should be caught with the fingers up and low pitches caught with the fingers down. The glove hand is soft, receiving the ball and gently pulling it back to the chest. Don't stab at it.

The catcher's free hand should be behind his back or behind his leg. Some kids put it behind the glove, and that is certainly less dangerous than keeping it exposed. I like it behind the back; I've seen too many bad bruises otherwise. It can get hit by the bat or by a foul tip. Keeping the hand behind some part of the body, fist clenched, protects it.

One of the most important things a catcher does is to control the pitcher's tempo and his emotions. She should constantly talk to the pitcher, reminding him to keep pitching "over the top," instead of relaxing into a sidearm motion, and to follow through when he starts getting tired. She should remind the pitcher to drive hard off the back foot. The catcher should keep reminding the pitcher of the catcher's glove—"hit the glove, here it is, pop the glove, baby." The catcher should pound the glove with her free hand, move the glove around a little bit, open and close it, anything to get the pitcher to focus on the glove. The catcher should sometimes yell out "nice pitch" on a strike, even before the umpire calls it. If the ball is a bit out of the strike zone, a quick snatch pulling the glove back into the strike zone can buy a strike sometimes. The catcher should slow the pitcher's rate of pitching if he starts to rush, particularly if the ball starts regularly coming in high. Stand up, walk around, slow the pitcher down so he takes time to concentrate.

If the catcher sees someone out of position he should tell them or tell the coach.

The second most important thing a catcher does is stop the low pitch. A pitch in the dirt is tough to catch, so the priority is to block it. Tell your child to drop to her knees, drop the glove low, fingers down, and concentrate on blocking the ball. If it goes into the glove, fine. It will at least be nearby. If the pitch is low and to one side, drop the closest knee in front of the ball and try to keep the body facing forward to help if the ball comes up. (See figure 5-2.)

If your child is a catcher, ask the coach if you can borrow the gear or keep it at home for the season. With this you can practice catching low pitches. Put some extra padding on the exposed areas

FIGURE 5-2

## BLOCKING LOW PITCHES

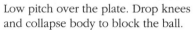

Low pitch over the plate. Drop knees and collapse body to block the ball.

Low pitch to one side. Lean, drop the knee to block, smother the ball.

such as the thighs and arms. Throw low pitches from about half the distance to the mound. Use a hard but rubber-coated ball at first. Make sure the chin is down to cover the neck and throat, and make double sure the throat guard is attached to the mask.

Another very important thing a catcher does is to throw out people who are stealing. Usually in Little League a kid steals only on a passed ball or wild pitch. So a good practice drill is to get the catcher in a crouch position and throw the ball behind him to the backstop. He then should turn, run to the ball, take off his mask as he runs and throw it to the side, pick the ball up and turn, firing the ball to second base. Practice this a dozen or so times each practice. After a while he will know how much time he has taken to get to the ball and whether he will have a play. Have a base runner run from first to second so timing can be learned. If the runner is stealing third, the catcher must be sure he has a play before throwing the ball. A bad throw will cost a run. This play, above all, should be practiced. Many coaches practice the throw to second, but the throw to third is more important. When a runner steals home on a passed ball, the catcher really needs to move quickly. He runs to the ball and snatches it to the pitcher covering home plate. It must be all one motion, and if it's done quickly the runner can be tagged.

An important job of catchers is to be able to get the runner out

FIGURE 5-3
## PLAY AT THE PLATE

Awaiting the throw: Place left foot just inside the plate as the ball approaches (not too early!). Proper tag position: In front of plate, left leg blocking plate, two hands on the ball, bring the right knee and glove down quickly and tag low. Brace the body for a collision.

at the plate. Usually the ball is thrown to them hurriedly, off line or in the dirt. Let catchers practice getting throws in the dirt, so they learn how to stop a bad throw. They should stand right in front of home plate, and if the ball is going to get to them, they turn and block the plate with the left foot, catch the ball with two hands (it must be two hands, a collision is coming), and bring the glove downward quickly to tag the feet. The runner must slide, or he is out, so the tag will always be low. The catcher should have her mask off; in fact, the mask should come off automatically every time the ball is hit. It's a lot easier to catch a ball at the plate if you can see it, so get the mask off. (See figure 5-3.)

A catcher should also practice catching foul tips (throw the ball straight up), and throwing to first base on bunts. Tell her to make sure she has an open angle to the first baseman so she doesn't hit the runner in the back. The key is to approach the ball from the left side and, if necessary, take a few steps toward the pitcher before throwing. Catchers also need to get used to picking the ball up as it is hit. It's difficult, but the idea is to look up quickly.

## FIRST BASE

I played a lot at first base over the years. I was tall, had a decent glove, was not very fast, and I could hit. These are good ingredients

FIGURE 5-4

# FIRST BASEMAN'S STRETCH

Both feet by the bag, determine the path of the ball before stretching. Then stretch. Don't overstretch. Step toward the throw.

for a first baseman. Add in a lefty, and it's perfect. A lefty doesn't have to rotate after getting to the bag to get the glove hand out to the throw like a righty does. A lefty also has an easier throw to second base.

In Little League play, first base is very important. Your whole infield is as good as your first baseman. The shortstop can make a great play, a good throw, but if the first baseman drops the ball or comes off the bag too early, the fielding effort was worthless. It happens countless times in youth league play! If your child can catch hard line drives, he or she can play at first.

A first baseman has one critical job—to catch the ball when it's thrown to him. When a grounder is hit to another infielder, the first baseman must spring to the bag quickly. He doesn't have to watch the ball; he has to look at the bag and get to it quickly. He must be ready for the throw and present a good target for the throw. When he gets to the bag, he puts the ball of his back foot's toe, the foot opposite his glove hand, on the inside edge of the bag and faces the fielder with the glove chest high. He doesn't stretch yet, not until he sees where the ball is going. Then he steps toward the ball, stretching only as far as he needs to, to catch the ball for the out.

(See figure 5-4.) If the play is not close and the ball is well thrown, the first baseman may need only a small step to catch the ball with two hands. However, in youth play the distance to first base is not great, so many plays are close, and a stretch may be needed. If the ball is thrown off line, a long stretch may be needed.

If the throw is bad, the primary job is to stop the ball from going through to the fence. If the first baseman can do that while touching the bag, swell, but if she has to leave the bag to catch the ball she must do so. Otherwise, the batter will go to second base and be in scoring position.

The toughest ball for a first baseman to catch, as with the catcher, is one in the dirt. Even a good fielder is handicapped by the fact that the foot must stay on the bag, which limits agility and reflexes. I used to practice catching balls thrown in the dirt with full catcher's gear on and a "cup." This eliminated my fear of a bad hop into my face, chest or neck. Practicing with a rubber-coated ball also helps. I learned to keep my head down, eyes on the ball. I could develop concentration and a sense for what the ball would do. First basemen have the biggest glove in the field, and that helps. I've seen first basemen who can stretch into a full split; that really looks sharp if you can do it.

If the throw is wide to the left, the first baseman's first thought should be to catch the ball and then tag the runner, sweeping the glove to the left.

In Little League many throws are high. The first baseman should practice the timing needed to jump for the ball. If it's clearly out of reach, he should not waste time looking at it, but turn and run to where it will go—he could stop the runner from advancing to second. He should make sure he doesn't collide with the runner, though. The runner will be going full speed, and that can hurt.

When a grounder is hit to the first baseman, or between her and the second baseman, she must always try to get it. I've seen many grounders go between the two fielders because the first baseman hesitates, feeling she had to cover the bag. On a grounder like that, the pitcher has to cover first base. The first baseman should always, always try to make the field play. It's good to practice the lob from the first baseman to the pitcher. It's a tough play for the pitcher, since he is on the run and must look for the ball, then find the bag.

The idea is to get the ball to the pitcher covering first as soon as possible. Hold the ball so the pitcher can see it and lob it to his glove. Keep the arm fairly straight, and lead the pitcher as much as is needed.

The first baseman also has to be ready to catch foul pops to the left side. The dugouts and fences are quite close, so she needs to practice knowing where they are.

A nerve-wracking play for the first baseman occurs when a runner is on third. I remember a play I was involved in when the shortstop got a grounder, looked at the runner on third to hold him there, and then threw to me. It was the tying run in the game, and just as the shortstop started to throw to me, the runner on third broke for home, and he was fast. Out of the corner of my eye I saw him running, and I sensed that he might beat my throw home, so I came off the bag, went to the ball, caught it and threw home. It was a smart play, my coach told me. The runner would surely have beaten the throw otherwise—it was just too bad I threw the ball over the backstop!

Once the batter goes to second base, the first baseman is free to do whatever he thinks is needed. Here it's likely the ball was hit to the fence, so the first baseman can run toward the center of the infield and get in line to back up any relays or act as a cutoff. As noted in chapter three, I like the pitcher to be the cutoff on most plays to the plate, since he is not needed behind the catcher in youth level play. The backstop is close enough to back up the catcher. However, on shots to the fence the pitcher usually backs up third base, since the batter will get to second base and threaten third base. The first baseman can run in to be the cutoff for any play at the plate. Otherwise he can back up the catcher. If the ball will be thrown to second base, he must stay and back up that throw. That's about it. Life at first base is really pretty simple.

## SECOND BASE

In Little League, particularly under age eleven, the second baseman gets the most grounders, not the shortstop. The shortstop does not even get the second most; the pitcher gets the second most grounders. The shortstop gets the third most plays, and the first baseman is right there with him.

Younger kids get the bat around slowly and drop the right side, so most balls go to the right side—right at the second baseman. Kids tend to play too close to the bag at second, but the proper positioning is about a third of the way to first base and 8 feet outside of the baseline.

A second baseman has to be able to stop grounders. She doesn't need a good arm (players with good arms go to shortstop or third), but she does need to be quick. She's got to run the grounders down, at least knock them down, so she can throw to first. The second baseman needs to be smart, too. There is much action, and you want somebody who can think.

When I think of second basemen, I think of smaller players. Good glove, quick, don't need a good arm. Remember, in baseball anybody of any size, speed or strength can play—if he is willing to practice and develop some simple skills. I had a kid two years ago named Danny, one of the smallest kids in the league. He couldn't throw hard and couldn't hit the ball out of the infield, but he was tough, and he wanted to play ball. He played with his friends every day. He played second base and did a good job.

Chapter three discussed infielding generally: the need to stay low, weight forward, knees bent, head down on the ball, eyes on the ball, glove on the ground raised forward to the ball in a scooping motion. An infielder has to be able to dance, up on the toes. She springs to the ball and hops into her throwing stance. If you look at the pros, they are always dancing around out there. And an infielder has to want the ball, hope it gets hit to her, and think about where she will throw it, before the ball is ever pitched. Talk to your players about these things; read the key points of this book to them, a little at a time; and then repeat the key phrases in this paragraph while you throw grounders to them.

Second basemen must know what to do with the ball when they get it. If there is nobody on, they throw to first. With a runner on first, they throw to the shortstop for the force at second. If the second baseman is close to the bag, he takes a step and lobs the ball to the shortstop. If he is farther away, he pivots on his toes and throws sidearm.

If a runner is on first and the ball is hit to the left side, the second baseman goes to the outfield side of second base to catch the throw from the shortstop or third baseman, then steps on second and sees if she can get the ball to first for a double play. If the runner is sliding, the second baseman may need to hop over him to avoid being undercut. This hop and throw is one of the most beautiful plays in all of baseball. It happens rarely in Little League so the second baseman needs to know how close the batter is to first.

There are several ways to pivot on second base, depending on timing and the situation. You can practice these by changing the timing and speed of your throw. If the runner is too close to first for a play, the second baseman should hold onto the ball—he doesn't want to throw it away. If there are runners on first and second, same thing—look for the force at second. Get the sure out. There are times you want to go to third I suppose, but Little League players should go for the out.

With bases loaded and less than two outs, the coach has a choice on what to do with infield grounders. In a close game, I always say throw home if you think you can stop the run—that's baseball, that's defense. Some coaches may not have faith in the catcher, or the second baseman's arm, and will still want the sure out at second base. My approach is to teach them right, but different people have different views about what is right and about winning.

If there is a runner on third, and she is not forced to run home, then the infielder gives her a look before throwing for the force at second or first. If the runner is going, then the infielder should throw home and get her out. Again, the purpose of defense is to stop runs. I say that's the way the game should be taught.

The second baseman is also the primary receiver of pop-ups for his side of the field, covering the space between the pitcher and first baseman. On any pop-up behind the pitcher or significantly behind the first baseman, the second baseman should get to the ball and call for it. The toughest catches are "Texas-leaguers"— shallow pops to the outfield. The second baseman has to turn and run, timing a leap for the ball. Practice these.

The second baseman is also the cutoff for outfield singles if the ball is hit to his side of the outfield and no one is on base. Read chapter three for the cutoffs when runners are on base. Almost any time a runner is on first or second base, the second baseman's responsibility on a single is to cover second base. Other players will cut off throws to third or home. Now, if the ball is hit deep, past the outfielder to the fence, then the second baseman must go out to assist the relay. He is not technically a cutoff at that point, he is just going out to make a relay.

On steals, I usually have the second baseman back up the short-stop on the throw from the catcher. In the big leagues, it depends on whether the batter is righty or lefty and where the ball might be hit. Usually on a righty batter the second baseman covers for the steal, because the ball will more likely be hit to the shortstop, and you want her to stay put while the runner at first is breaking for second. But in Little League the kid can't steal till the ball gets to the batter, so the situation is not the same. I think the shortstop can see the play better from her position. She can see the runner, so I let her make the tag. The second baseman backs her up.

Finally, the second baseman covers first base on bunts to the right side. The first baseman goes for the bunt, and someone needs to cover first base. The shortstop will cover second base.

## SHORTSTOP

I'm not going to repeat everything I said in chapter three and sum-marized for the preceding section on second basemen. Much of the material about second basemen also pertains to shortstops.

By the time kids are playing "major league" baseball (in Little League eleven- and twelve-year-olds play in the "major league"), the shortstop becomes the cornerstone of the defense. She has to have a good glove, because the batters start to get around on the ball and more balls get hit to that position. She also has to have a good arm, because it's the longest infield throw, even longer than for the third baseman (if they are playing the right positions), and she has to hurry the throw to beat the runner. A shortstop assist is a pretty thing to see at Little League level. Often the throw is late or high. Shortstop is another position for natural leaders.

A shortstop is usually the natural athlete who is born ready to play. He can do it all, and at that position you need it all. Most teams put their best all-around player at shortstop (when he is not pitching). This doesn't mean your son or daughter can't play short-stop, it just means he or she has to be the best if they want to play shortstop. And as I noted earlier, you don't have to be born with it. Plenty of kids who are just average athletes work daily on their skills and become good enough to do the job. Yes, any child can learn to do anything in baseball.

Since shortstops should usually play as deep "in the hole" as possible (that's about 12 feet back from the baseline toward the outfield), they face a long throw. So more than any other infielder, the shortstop has to make the transition from fielding to throwing as quickly as possible. This transition involves two moves. The first is to get the ball out of the glove into the throwing hand, and the second is to hop into a set throwing position. (See chapter three on throwing positions.) So when you practice for shortstop, focus on making the transition quickly. Talk about the need for quickness and practice the transition repeatedly.

With a runner on first, I like the shortstop to try to make the double play himself. If he is too far from second base he obviously must throw the ball, but on a shot to his left the shortstop should think about doing it himself. The throw to the second baseman always runs the risk of being a problem. The second baseman takes time to change directions, and his throw is often off balance. If the shortstop does it himself, these risks are eliminated. I know that this is not so on the big league fields, but this is one of the several things that are different for the smaller fields. Big league shortstops are too far from the bag to make double plays by themselves.

It's the same way with the cutoff situation on a short single with no one on base. I like the outfielder to throw directly to the base, that is, the so-called cutoff stands on second base. For a ball hit to the left, the shortstop is the cutoff and the second baseman backs him up. They switch roles for a ball hit to the right. This is because the throw is so short, the outfielder can reach easily. I've always seen coaches send out a cutoff on a throw toward second, and the cutoff is 10 feet from the outfielder. It doesn't make sense to do a cutoff just to do a cutoff. The game always has to make sense, and in Little League you have to adjust a bit, particularly for eleven- and twelve-year-olds.

The shortstop has all shallow pop-ups on her side of the diamond and behind the third baseman. She plays deeper than the third baseman and can cover behind the third baseman more easily. Obviously, the fielder always has to call for the ball. Players should not rush to call too early, but the shortstop's call is law.

As far as calling for the ball goes, I am a bit of a renegade here. Many coaches teach that the first player who calls for a ball gets it. I teach that the second player, or last player, who calls for the ball gets it, but he has to call off the first player very loudly and repeatedly. I do this for several reasons. First, the first one who calls often does so too soon, out of instinct. Second, the wind can change circumstances very quickly. Third, the second caller had more time to make a judgment that his position is better. This doesn't mean that he is a better catcher, just that he is in a better position, and he is calling the first player off. In any event, if two players call for the ball, someone has to get it, and the rule should be a firm one either way.

The coach may set some general rules of priority on calling the ball, although I've rarely seen coaches do this at the Little League level. For instance, the center fielder has priority over anybody, an outfielder has priority over an infielder, a shortstop and second baseman have priority over other infielders on their side of the infield, the catcher has priority over no one (because the catcher's mitt is not made for pop-ups). Obviously, players should not be too quick to call for the ball, and they must make sure it will land in their territory.

As with second basemen, if there is an unforced player on second or third, the shortstop should see if the runner is going and fake a throw to hold him on base before he throws to first. The shortstop fake on this play, again, has to be the quickest of all, because he barely has time to get the ball to first as it is. Sometimes, all he will have time for is to give the runner a sharp look. This is a good move to practice a few times. Have the shortstop fake a throw to third and then throw to first. Remember, he has to work on quickness or he will lose the runner at first.

The shortstop is the cutoff for long singles to the left side with no one on, although I usually tell her to just stand 10 feet in front of second, with the second baseman backing her up on the bag. With a runner on first, the throw should go to third to stop the lead runner, and the shortstop is the cutoff for all three outfielders. She must line up between the ball and third base, about 15 to 20 feet from the bag. She has to know where the runner is, and if the batter heads for second base, the shortstop has to decide whether to cut the ball off and throw to second or let the ball go through for a play at third. Obviously, if the throw is off line, there will be no play at third, so the shortstop must cut the ball off.

On any ball hit past the outfielder on his side, the shortstop must go out far enough to get the relay throw, and he should know what he's going to do with the ball when he gets it—this is where the other infielders can help by telling the shortstop where to go. They should be looking at the runners to figure it out.

## THIRD BASE

Usually, the fewest number of balls are hit to third base in Little League. In the pros it's called the "hot corner," but not in Little League. That's because the batters don't have much bat speed, so they tend to hit more to the right side. This is fine with me because it gives me a chance to use third base to try out different kids at infielding. It's also a place to put a kid who may be a bit weak defensively but whose bat is too good to leave out of the lineup.

Third base is also good for a kid who may have a decent glove, good reflexes, but is too slow to play shortstop or second. A third baseman must have a good arm to reach first base on grounders and the ability to catch a throw from the catcher on runners stealing third. The second is more important. If the third baseman misses the throw, the runner goes home, if the local rules allow it. This must be practiced. The third baseman should straddle the back of the bag and bring the ball down very quickly to a spot six inches in front of the bag and make the tag. (See figure 5-5.)

One way to practice this play is to tell your player she doesn't have to stand on the bag. Often kids think they have to have a foot on the bag, and this reduces their mobility. They should straddle the back of the bag, facing the catcher. They must know that catching the ball, wherever it is, is more important than tagging the runner. Once she catches the ball, the next move is to bring the glove down quickly to the side of the base for the tag. The runner must slide!

The third baseman, like the first baseman, should know where the sideline fence is, for purposes of chasing down foul pop-ups. For practice you can throw some pop-ups close to the fence. Tell

FIGURE 5-5
## TAGGING A RUNNER

Straddle base, bend knees, block base with glove letting runner slide into low glove.

the third baseman to see where the ball is going, head in that direction, take a quick glance at where the fence or dugout is, adjust accordingly, and then look again at the ball. It feels very awkward at first to take your eye off the ball, but it's not so bad after practicing it a few times.

I tell the third baseman to play in close. Since the ball usually is not hit hard to third in Little League, grounders are often slow. The kids don't have the bat speed yet. I'd back up the third baseman for stronger hitters, but other than that I want him on the fringe of the grass. He has to learn to charge the slow dribbler. If it's slow enough it can be picked up with one hand, but this is done only if needed to beat the runner to first. The idea, as with fielding any grounder, is to scoop the ball from behind rather than snatch it from above. This way it has less chance to roll under the hand.

The third baseman is never a cutoff. In the pros the third baseman is the cutoff for plays at the plate from the left side of the outfield, but not in Little League. Coaches must be practical. The third baseman guards an important bag, and I want him there. He doesn't go out for relays, the shortstop does that. On plays to home plate the pitcher or first baseman is my cutoff in Little League. If the pitcher is backing up third, then the first baseman comes in if he is free. Third basemen guard third base, that's it!

The essence of third base is diving for hot liners or grounders. The picture of Brooks Robinson, perhaps the best defensive player who ever lived, diving left or right for hard shots and then popping up for an amazing throw, is etched in the minds of fans everywhere. (See figure 5-6.) Tell your players that this is often what it takes. It's hard to practice, but it should be in their minds.

## OUTFIELD

In youth baseball left field is a very lonely position. I said it several times about other positions, but until players are about twelve they don't get the bat around quickly enough—the pitchers are too fast. The ball is usually hit to right or right center field. With my fast pitchers, I always put my best outfielder in right field. If I have a kid pitching who is slower, then I put my strength in center field. The right fielder, in any event, needs to be a decent catcher and has to have the strongest arm in the outfield to get the ball to third base. More on that later. Left field is a place to learn. There is not much action, not much pressure.

Chapter three addressed some general defensive hints and practice drills for outfielders. A key idea is to practice with soft balls, like tennis balls or rubber balls. Cork-filled balls are also good for this. The child should catch the ball above eye level, palm facing outward. The main idea is to get quickly to the ball and get under

FIGURE 5-6

## THE HOT CORNER

The defining move for third basemen. Concentrate on and time the ball, then dive and stab it. Knock it down if that's all you can do.

it: Set to catch, and set to make the transition to throw the ball. Also, on a ball over the head, the outfielder should turn and run, not back up. I also talked about throwing ahead of the lead runner and hitting the cutoff. A brief summary follows for a ball hit in front of the outfielder, that is, not a deep shot:

1. No one on. Get the ball to second base. Hit the cutoff, the shortstop or the second baseman, depending on what side of the field you are on. The cutoff should be standing on the base if the

throw will be relatively short, or about 10 to 15 feet in front of the base for longer throws.

2. Man on first. Throw the ball toward third base. Make sure you hit the cutoff; it should be the shortstop.

3. Men on first and second. Throw home toward the cutoff in the middle of the infield. It should be the pitcher or first baseman. The pitcher will cut the ball off if the runner on second stops at third.

4. Man on second or men on second and third. Same as #3, except now the batter will look to go to second, so the cutoff has to work well.

5. Man on third. Same as #1. As far as the outfield is concerned there is nobody on, since the runner on third will score by the time the outfielder has the ball.

6. Bases loaded. Same as #3. The runner on third will score; it's the runner on second you want to stop; he is the lead runner for outfield purposes.

Also, if the ball is hit over the outfielder's head or through the gap to the fence, he should go get it as fast as he can. It will be a long throw, so shortstop or second base may have to come out to help. Don't look around! If the outfielder is too far away to throw anybody out, he should get the ball to the relay and let him "shoot" somebody. If there was no one on, then the throw should be toward third base, since the batter will easily get to second base. If there was a runner on first, he is a definite scoring threat, and the throw must head home, since he will easily get to third (unless he is quite slow). Remember, it's important to have general rules and it's also important to know that there are exceptions. Play the game on the field.

Chapter three didn't cover fielding outfield grounders. These are among the toughest fielding plays to make in baseball. The fields the kids play on are often not rolled in the springtime; the grass may be kept at varying lengths; there are often ruts, holes, rocks or grass clumps. The ball can take wicked bounces.

Fielders shouldn't charge a ground ball. Teach them to let it take a good bounce, and then, if there is no one on, to lower one knee

FIGURE 5-7
## FIELDING OUTFIELD GROUNDERS

A major problem arises when a ball scoots by an outfielder. Try to get directly in front of it and block the path with the lowered leg.

toward the ground. I like the knee barely touching the ground, so the fielder can come up quickly if the ball bounces wide. There is no substitute for lowering the knee. The transition from catching to throwing is not as important as it is in the infield, so the fielder makes sure to stop the ball, getting the body in front of it. (See figure 5-7.) Of course, with runners in scoring position, the outfielder needs to be more aggressive to get the ball quickly into the infield. However, even then he should be under control!

On steals, the center fielder backs up second base, and the left fielder backs up third base. The left fielder may not get many hits in his direction, but there will be many throws from the catcher to third, and many will get past the third baseman. On the pitch, the left fielder should hold his position until the ball passes the batter, and then get ready to break toward third base. If a runner goes, the left fielder does break toward third, heading obliquely to the foul line, to get there before the ball does. If the throw is wild, the left fielder must head where the ball is heading. He should not get too close to the third baseman, no closer than 25 feet. Otherwise, the ball could get by. (See figure 5-8.)

Finally, remember that runners will tag up on fly balls that the outfielders catch. An outfielder can't stand there gleaming over a

FIGURE 5-8

## BACKING UP THIRD BASE

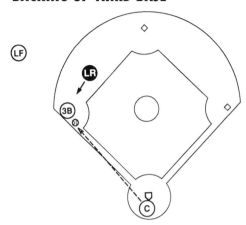

The left fielder must back up third base on throws from the catcher. Head to a point about twenty-five feet behind third base.

great catch—she must get the ball to the base in front of the lead runner. It is very hard to get a runner at the plate, but third base for left fielders and center fielders, and second base for the right fielder are good bets.

## PITCHER

Last but certainly not least! Pitching is about the same at any level of baseball. Whether a nine-year-old or a big leaguer, a good pitcher is simply more valuable than anything else. This is just a fact of baseball life. Championships are won at every level with good pitching.

This truth doesn't diminish by one iota my statement that hitting is the essence of baseball.

Hitting is for everybody, because everybody is a hitter. Pitching, however, is pretty much reserved for the gifted athletes. Some kids have a knack for getting the ball over the plate, and they just need to develop arm strength. Some have a gift for throwing hard, and they just need years of experience to gain control. A few rare ones have both at an early age, and their teams will simply always win. They can take pressure. These kids are the pitchers, the "chosen people" of baseball. (See figure 5-9.) A pitcher can be anyone who can throw hard; the fastball is the cornerstone of pitching. Control comes over time and is essential for a kid who doesn't throw very hard.

FIGURE 5-9
## THE PITCHER

The chosen few of baseball. Games are won with pitching heat and control.

This doesn't mean that your son or daughter is not a pitcher just because he or she can't hit the side of a barn from inside the barn. My youngest son had a strong arm but little control over his throws until he was eleven. After four years of organized Little League ball, he finally got some pitching innings. He *wanted* to pitch, and he practiced at it. It paid off, and I gave him a shot. Coaches will respond to desire. Joey may never be a top pitcher, but he earned some innings.

If you want to evaluate a child's pitching ability, just have him pitch to you and see how many strikes he throws and whether he throws hard. Most pitches should be quite close.

## Arm Burnout

You will know pretty quickly if a boy or girl is a potential pitcher. However, this is one point where I caution against too much practice. The shoulder and elbow muscles and tendons are placed under much stress when throwing a ball, and it is simply scandalous how many kids burn out their arms in Little League level play. They not only pitch at games and at practice, but, because good pitchers are so rare, they are called on by their friends to pitch in sandlot games. Big league pitchers get four days rest, yet kids at play often pitch nearly every day. Don't let it happen. Set rules and enforce them. During the season, ensure that a pitcher's arm gets rested. Above all, don't get out and practice pitching every day. I'd let Joey throw me a dozen or so pitches a few times a week, no more. The same holds true for any throwing at practice. You don't want too many hard throws a day, and you never throw hard until you have first had a few dozen soft throws to warm up.

## Pitching Style

OK, assuming you have a budding pitcher, what do you need to know about style? I'll discuss here the elements of a pitch, but the thing you start talking about right away is consistency. A good pitcher is a robot on the mound, throwing pretty much with the same movement every pitch. Your child must understand this immediately. (See figure 5-10.)

1. Address the Batter. Pitchers in Little League usually have a small mound with a rubber on it. Tell your child to step on the rubber with the right foot, toes overhanging the rubber, and face the batter. Don't look at the batter; look only at the catcher's mitt. Hands are at the side. The left foot is slightly behind the right foot, to the left of the rubber. The pitcher should stand in the same spot on the rubber each time. Most kids want to lean forward a bit, but the key is to be comfortable. If there is no rubber, have the pitcher draw one on the dirt, or make some mark. Pitchers must start thinking about consistency.

2. The Windup. The windup is essentially a stretching motion, raising both hands up, usually over the head, then bringing the hands together as they are lowered, and finally coming to a complete stop. The pitcher starts a rocking motion forward and then straight back a half step as he raises his hands.

3. The Crane. After the pitcher rocks back, he turns or pivots his right foot astride (still touching) the rubber and lifts his left leg for balance. At the same time he drops his hands and reaches back

FIGURE 5-10

## SIX PARTS OF THE PITCH

Address the Batter. Start from same spot and position, consistency is key. Grip ball with fingers, ball away from palm, hands at side, take a breath.

The Windup. Rock the body, step to front of rubber slowly turning right foot, raise hands over head.

with his right (pitching) hand towards second base, extending his right arm straight back and downward. Lifting the left leg resembles a crane (bird) standing on one leg.

4. The Kick. At this point the pitcher rocks forward again, lunging his body, driving toward the batter. He drives hard and low with the back leg for power, whips open his front shoulder, and kicks out the front leg.

5. The Delivery. The throwing arm should be extended and driven forward by the snap of the hip, shoulder, elbow and wrist. The body is brought down hard with the front foot. The ball is released as high as possible.

6. The Follow-Through. As a natural consequence of forward and downward rotation, the pitching hand follows through the ball toward the ground.

FIGURE 5-10 (cont.)

## SIX PARTS OF THE PITCH

The Crane. Lift front knee straight up while rotating body back on back leg a bit, hand overhead, look at catcher's glove.

The Kick. Reach straight back with ball, kick front leg out towards batter, stretch, drive hard with back leg, lunge towards batter.

The Delivery. Whip open the left shoulder, extend the throwing arm, keep elbow up, throw over the top, open up hips and come down hard with front foot.

The Follow-Through. Follow through fully, gracefully. Stay low, let the drive foot naturally swing forward to regain balance and prepare for a play.

## Pitching Tips

Now for some pitching tips. Here are some more things to look for and emphasize:

1. I mentioned consistency. You want the pitching style to look the same each time. Talk about this idea. It is not a combination of different moves but one continuous, smooth, but explosive action. Talk about gracefulness and smoothness. Also talk about power.

2. Reaching the arm down and straight back just before the delivery promotes full extension early in the pitch and prevents erratic movement at that critical moment. If the arm drifts off to first or third base slightly, this can throw it off. One pro pitcher told me he liked to reach toward his back pocket with the ball, just to start at the same point each time.

3. Most pros lift their knee in the crane position at least waist high, and sometimes chest high. This adds power by forcing the body to rock back farther, but it can take some time for a youngster to adjust to the control needed. Some kids get into the bad habit of merely sweeping their left foot back toward second base, rather than lifting it, and that's a habit that must be corrected at once.

4. The delivery should be over the top, arm and ball as high as possible. To avoid sidearm throws, it is of highest importance to keep the elbow up, higher than the shoulder. Kids sometimes go to sidearm when they are tired or because they feel it gives more control. Sure, we've all seen good sidearm pitchers. Bret Saberhagen was one of the best relievers in the game in the early 1980s, and he threw sidearm/underhanded. But encourage your son or daughter to come over the top, or at least at a three-quarter (270 degree) angle. This produces a more powerful pitch, and it's better for longevity of the arm, since the motion is not as herky-jerky as the sidearm throw.

5. The grip was covered in chapter three. Two fingers on the top, crossing the threads. Thumb on the left, and ring and pinkie fingers on the right, cradling the ball. The two top fingers should be fairly close together. The pitcher holds the ball with the fingers; it does not touch the palm, and there should be a space in the thumb pocket. (See figure 5-11.)

FIGURE 5-11
## FASTBALL GRIP

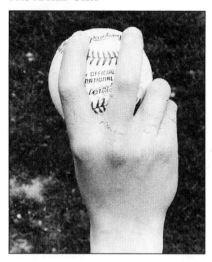

Fingertips over seam, ball not too deep into palm.

6. I talked about driving with the back foot, pushing off the end of the rubber. Much power can be added from the back foot. The pitcher should be told to try to draw from this driving power and relay the power into the pitch. It's a matter of perception.

7. The left foot kicks out toward home and should land on the left side of an imaginary line from the back foot to the middle of the plate. This is called "opening up the door." The left foot, left shoulder and left arm can be perceived as a door, opening up to the pitch. Often pitchers don't open up enough, stepping *on* rather than *past* the imaginary line, and the left foot then interferes with the follow-through. I teach my pitchers to first perceive they are driving their left shoulder at the batter, and then open it up and swing the door. Avoid opening up too soon, losing power and control. The left foot should point to the plate when it lands and not come down at an angle to the plate. Also, the left foot should come down hard, pulling the pitcher into a complete follow-through.

Al Santorini was probably the best high school pitcher New Jersey ever had and pitched for a good number of years in the pros. Al, now a Little League coach, told me that very few coaches realize the importance of landing hard with the stretch foot.

Finally, the stretch should be fairly long. A long stretch brings the body's center of gravity down, so the pitch comes down too. Low and outside pitches are the best pitches. The foot should land squarely, as flat as possible, trying not to jerk the body too much.

8. I've mentioned the follow-through a few times. You should talk about it. A follow-through is a result of a good drive and stretch and should happen automatically because of forward momentum. If a player has to try to follow through, he just doesn't have enough forward momentum. The pitcher snaps his wrist downward, making the ball spin, but also causing the follow-through. Lack of follow-through is a good sign that the wrist is not snapping.

## Pitching Strategy

At the younger ages the strategy is simple—just get the ball over the plate. The pitcher who gives up the most walks will lose. At the older youth ages, you can begin to discuss some strategy.

1. Take your time. Too often the kids rush from one pitch to the next. They need to develop a rhythm, and they need to focus on concentration. When you start seeing high pitches, that's a good time to slow the pitcher down.

2. Hit the glove. The catcher's glove is the whole world to the pitcher. He should blank everything out except thinking about the glove and trying to hit it. As control comes, the pitcher should think about corners of the glove. He must focus on the glove at all times, and during every part of the pitch.

3. Get in front of the batter. The first strike is important. If you get two strikes and no balls or one ball, then rear back and fire some heat! Don't let a batter beat you when you are ahead. You can afford to give up some control in favor of heat when you are ahead in the count.

4. Know the batters. If a batter won't swing, throw easy strikes. Fire heat at the good hitters.

5. If a ball is hit to the pitcher's left side, the pitcher must always break to cover first base. If he is not needed, he can stop.

6. If the lead runner is on first base, the pitcher backs up third. If the lead runner is on second, the pitcher is the cutoff at the plate.

On a passed ball or wild pitch with a runner on third, the pitcher covers the plate.

7. Since the pitcher has the best view of the action on a hit ball, he or she should take charge on helping fielders with where to throw the ball.

8. In Little League, pitchers can pitch only six innings a week, Sunday to Saturday. They must have at least one day of rest between appearances and must rest three full days if they pitch more than three innings in a game.

9. With runners on base the pitcher uses a set position if runners can steal. The pitcher stands sideways in front of the rubber, with the back foot sidling to the rubber.

## Types of Pitches

As noted earlier, the fastball is the bread and butter of pitching. At young ages it is pretty much the only pitch used. It's just a hard straight pitch. If the ball is gripped across the seams as in figure 5-11, it will go straight, and even rise a bit as your child gets stronger. The great pitchers throw rising fastballs—an extremely difficult pitch to hit with a bat moving in a downward arc. If your child wants some variety, tell him or her to hold the ball along and on top of the two seams where they come together. This will cause the ball to sink a bit.

The curveball is the second most popular pitch, but kids rarely throw curves before high school. Coaches don't know how to teach it, and that's good because it's tougher on the arm than a fastball if it is thrown wrong. The main idea is to throw more with the middle finger and to snap and turn the wrist sharply, giving the ball a sideways spin. As the wrist snaps it turns in toward the body. It is essential to keep the elbow up. You can try it, but don't concentrate on it.

Other pitches are sliders, split-finger fastballs, knuckleballs and change-ups. The change-up is an interesting pitch. The ball is set back into the palm with the fingers loose on top of the ball. The wrist snap is not used, and the ball is launched with centrifugal force. The change-up is an important pitch to have with a good fastball. Let your child learn these in high school. He'll kill his arm trying to learn them too early. Besides, some local rules forbid "funny" pitches.

*Chapter Six*

# RUNNING A PRACTICE

Perhaps the most common question I get from parents who begin to coach a baseball team is, "How do I start?", or "How do I run a practice?" The short answer is have them hit baseballs until their arms fall off. The long answer follows.

Well, the job starts the day you agree to coach! A few weeks before the first practice, at least a month, you should get the word out to your team and to their parents that things will go much better if the players show up in decent shape. Baseball doesn't require the endurance of most other sports, but it does require strength, quickness and agility. I feel it's best, particularly at grade school levels, to suggest that the players come to practice able to run a half-dozen 50-yard wind sprints without looking like they are about to collapse and able to do twenty-five to fifty pushups. Younger kids won't have the upper body strength, but they can get started. Have them do what they can, and then strive for *just one more*! This means they should work at least every other day up to this level.

The other thing kids need to do early is learn the basics of the game. Kids learn to understand baseball at a very young age in this country, but don't assume too much. Tell parents about this book! It's written for parents as much as for coaches, and parents can be a great help to you if they get involved early on in explaining the game and instructing their child.

Unfortunately, you probably will not get as much practice time as you want or need. There are many more teams than fields. Early in the season there is not much daylight and plenty of April showers. Teams customarily get to practice a couple of times a week at best. An enterprising coach can find a way to get more practice, but it's not the rule.

Clearly the best practice condition is on a regulation field with smoothed out dirt surfaces. But any open field will do for batting, pitching and outfield practice. A parking lot or light traffic road is fine for infield practice. A trip to the batting cages is an excellent alternative to a rained-out practice. Videotape the kids batting, pitching and fielding, then plan an evening at someone's house to view the tapes, maybe with some pizza.

There are many ways to enrich a practice schedule, even if you just urge mom, dad or big brother to spend thirty minutes having a catch. Advise them to throw some grounders and pop-ups (throw left, right, then deep) or to work on batting form. The no pitch drill, described later, is a great form drill and requires no special area, just a net or link fence to hit balls against. The more you get your players drilling their skills, the better your team will be. That's just the surest thing about any sport! A coach must find creative ways to get players more practice time. Sure, you may not be able to spend every night on it, but that's where parents and assistant coaches come in.

There are several key objectives that you need to consider for each practice plan. Their relative importance will vary a bit as you get further into the season, and they also vary depending on what age group you work with, but these concepts are always important and should be part of your plan for each practice.

## FIVE KEY GOALS OF THE PRACTICE

1. Get the players in shape.
2. Understand each player's potential.
3. Work on individual skills: batting, baserunning and defensive skills for each position.
4. Work on team execution of defensive plays.
5. Motivate, communicate, lead.

Baseball practices typically last two to three hours, depending on day of the week and amount of daylight. All five goals listed above should be considered each time you prepare a practice plan (I'll get to what a practice plan looks like a bit later).

In a two-hour practice, I would devote ten minutes to chatter and water breaks, twenty minutes to conditioning, sixty minutes to batting practice, thirty minutes to defensive skills development, and thirty minutes to team dynamics. Doesn't add up? It does if you can do a few things at the same time! In fact, if you have many parent-coaches helping out you can literally double each of these time frames.

Early in the season you should spend more time on conditioning, speed, agility drills and batting. Later in the season you need to spend more time on specialty drills for refinements such as cutoffs, bunts, pick-offs, rundowns and baserunning signs.

Let's look at each idea.

## Get the Players in Shape

Frankly, it doesn't take much to get grade-school or high-school kids into shape, and there is just no excuse when they aren't. Baseball does not require much endurance, but a lot of improvement can come from some strength training, speed drills and agility drills. The worst mistake is to assume that kids will get themselves into shape. Baseball coaches tend to underestimate the value of conditioning, but stronger kids hit longer balls. Even if you only get your kids to double the number of push-ups they can do, they will be better hitters.

There are a few dos and don'ts about getting players in shape.

### Warming Up

Make sure players warm up before practice. A few laps around the field at a slow pace should break a sweat and warm up major leg muscles. Of special concern early in the season are the large muscles high on the inner thigh and in the groin area. Most ballplayers have experienced strains here, usually while running down to first base, and these strains can take weeks to heal. Tell your players that muscles are like bubble gum—unless they stretch slowly they will tear. After stretching, the kids should pair up and have a catch to loosen up their arms and elbows. Tell them to get there a few minutes early each time so they can warm up before practice.

Don't expect that players will warm up sufficiently on their own. They should be told to stretch it out on their own before practice, but then get the team together to do it some more. Players get hurt too easily when they're not loose, and *you* need to see that it gets done.

Start the team off with what I call the Quick Cali Set: twenty-five jumping jacks, twenty-five push-ups, fifteen half sit-ups, a dozen toe touches with legs crossed, twenty trunk turns, and several major leg stretches.

Then do the Leg Stretch Set. Leg stretches should be done smoothly without jerking or straining. A few good ones are:

1. Toe-hand: lying on the back with arms outstretched, alternately touch each foot to the opposite hand.
2. Hurdler: sitting on the ground with one leg forward and one bent backward, touch the forward toe, then slowly lean back, stretching the back leg (reverse legs and repeat).
3. Standing quadricep: standing on one foot, grasp the other foot behind the back and gently pull it to the buttocks, half dozen for each leg of each exercise.
4. Supine hamstring: lying on the back, pull each leg alternately to the chest.
5. Thigh stretch: standing with legs outstretched, lean to one side, bending that knee, stretching the opposite thigh muscle.
6. Achilles and calf stretch: place one foot a step in front of the other, lean forward and bend the front leg, stretching the lower part of the back leg (reverse and do other leg). No jerking movements, no bobbing up and down!

The captain can lead the exercises, and you can let him or her start this part of the practice while you get organized, check to see who is there, talk to coaches or parents. (See figure 6-1.)

Monitor your players. Evaluate the heat at all times when doing conditioning, and make sure none of the players gets heat exhaustion, especially late in the season when it's hot.

Don't overwork players! Some coaches have their kids running all the time all season long. The players are young, but there are limits even for the young.

By the same token, there can be periods when players are just standing around. I believe that push-ups are the best single exercise for building upper body strength in kids (along with the hated sit-ups). Hand out sets of twenty push-ups or sit-ups freely. Tell the kids when it's not punishment (and when it is).

Another great strength enhancer to use at practice is what I call the *wrist machine*. It's simply a two-foot section of broom handle or thick pipe with four feet of clothesline attached to the center and

FIGURE 6-1

# LEG STRETCHES

Toe-Hand. Lying on the back with arms outstretched, alternately touch each foot to the opposite hand.

Hurdler. Sitting on the ground with one leg forward and one bent backward, touch the forward toe, then slowly lean back, stretching the back leg.

FIGURE 6-1 (cont.)

## LEG STRETCHES

Thigh Stretch. Standing with legs out-stretched, lean to one side, bending that knee, stretching the opposite thigh muscle.

Achilles and Calf Stretch. Place one foot a step in front of the other, lean forward and bend the front leg, stretching the lower part of the back leg.

a five- to ten-pound weight attached to the other end of the line. The idea is to hold the bar with two outstretched hands, and coil or roll the bar and the line around it until the weight rises to reach the bar. Then lower it and do it twice more. This is great for wrists and forearms—key muscle groups for batting and throwing.

I had the kids use the wrist machine after they batted. Tell them that you are trying to give them an edge they will need when they come up against their opponents. A kid who does a hundred push-ups a day will become very strong! Judge what a player can do, and slightly push his limit. Don't ask him to do something that will embarrass him, though.

I generally recommend that you avoid formal weight training for grade-school kids. They are still growing at a rapid pace. There is a different view, however, and I'll present it in chapter eight.

Don't do wind sprints at the beginning of practice. They require the loosest muscles, so do them at the end of practice. Then do short ones, 5 to 10 yards at first, then 25 yards. Tell the players to reach out in a long stride. Do some backwards and some sideways.

Finish with a few 25-yard races. Wind sprints are essential for pitchers' leg strength.

### Speed Improvement Drills

You can't do much to make a slow kid a lot faster. But you can improve speed significantly, and you can improve running strength, agility and balance a good deal.

Some good drills to improve running speed and form are:

1. The Robot. Line up the players and have them run 40 yards at half speed, alternatively driving their fists down from neck height to just behind the buttocks. The idea is to bang or drive the fists downward in a robotic cadence in rhythm with their stride. Look at track stars in the 100-yard dash, and observe how they pump the arms. Have your players run it three times, increasing speed each time.

2. The Bounce. Similar to the drill above, but have them concentrate on lifting their knees high to the chest, bouncing off the ground with each step and lifting the knees as high as possible. This drill is routinely done by track stars and high jumpers. It develops the power thrust needed to sprint. Try to incorporate the first drill with the second after a while.

3. The Buttkick. Again run 40 yards and return, this time kicking the heels into the buttocks. This helps the follow-through needed for a complete stride. Every bit of thrust is needed to sprint.

4. The Goosestep. Finally, run 40 yards in a goosestep, kicking the legs straight out and lifting them straight and high. The idea here is to train to reach out for a greater stride.

### Agility Drills

1. Simon Says. Line up players in five lines. The first row of five starts running in place, in short, quick, choppy steps. The coach signals with his hand for the players to shuffle laterally (without crossing the feet), forward, backward, down to the ground and up again. Players must square the shoulders, stay low and react quickly. Slow reacting players who don't appear to be trying hard enough may be rewarded with a dozen push-ups.

2. Carioca. Lined up as above, players carioca, that is, run side-

ways, left foot over right, then left foot behind right, for 40 yards. Repeat four times.

## Understand Each Player's Potential

You need to figure out what each player can do, so each can concentrate on developing the specific skills for his or her position. Then you need to keep an open mind, and figure out which players you were wrong about. I've seen many coaches quickly decide who plays where and then never change it. Countless times I have seen a coach stick someone in an odd position late in a meaningless game and suddenly find that the kid is a natural there. While it's important to get things set early, so you can concentrate on the special skills required for each position (as discussed in chapter five), you should always be looking to see if someone can help the team somewhere else. Assistant coaches can help you a lot here.

A good tool in this respect is to start making lists. Run sprints to see who your fastest players are. Who can accelerate the fastest (short distance speed)? Who are the most agile? Who are the gutsiest players? Who are the strongest players? Who has the best hands? Once you create these lists, don't throw them away. Check them every couple of weeks to see if someone has earned another look.

The lists force you to evaluate your players according to different aspects of athletic ability. Sometimes you will be surprised to see a name pop up of a player you hadn't been looking at very closely. Constantly evaluate and reevaluate your players. It's incredible to me how rarely some coaches discuss each player. It is far too easy to overlook a quiet kid who may have good ability. An assistant coach usually has seen something that can surface in such a full review. Don't just label someone for the season. Reconsider constantly. Give a kid a shot at something else if she is not working out where you first placed her.

You will find many brief opportunities on the practice field to talk to your players. How is school? How are things at home? What are your interests? You can find out a lot about a kid in just a few minutes. This helps you understand the player, and you will also begin to earn his respect. Kids who like and respect you are more coachable.

## Work on Individual Skills

After fifteen to twenty minutes of conditioning, stretching, speed and agility drills, I like to call the players together. Tell them generally what they will be doing next and what you expect of them. Details can be supplied by assistant coaches later. You should focus on individual position skills and fundamentals.

I think it's a great idea to film kids at practice. Try to get a parent to volunteer to take some shots of players working on form—pitching, fielding, throwing. Circulate the tapes to kids who need to see what they are doing wrong. You can all meet at someone's house to view the films and talk about form. In coaching, as in art, a picture is truly worth a thousand words.

Working on form and fundamentals is essential. This must be done early in the season on a regular basis. If a shortstop's head comes up too soon, or if a batter's hands drop, or if the first baseman stretches too soon, let him know. If he doesn't get the message, fifteen push-ups will help him see your point. There is no excuse for poor form! A player may not be able to hit every pitch or execute every play well, but he can always employ proper form, and it will help! Have the checklist at the end of the book handy to check out form.

I usually divide the team into two groups for defensive practice and batting practice. You don't need every player daydreaming out in the field during batting practice. Take seven kids off to bat, and let the others break up into even smaller groups for defensive or specialty practice.

Generally, outfielders bat while infielders work on defense, and vice versa. Since you need to move batting practice into the outfield area while infielders practice, use a sheet of plywood for a second backstop. The whole idea is to use practice time profitably so kids get a lot of repetition and don't get bored. Obviously, if you have no help and only a small playing area, there is only so much you can do. I always manage to figure out someway to keep everyone occupied, and I *always, always* get parents involved helping out.

### Defensive Practice

As noted, I like to break the players into small groups to work on individual skills. If you have several assistant coaches (get parents involved!), that's best since then you can float from group to group. If you don't have enough adults, have a player be captain of the group. The groups vary for different skills, so I'll list some of the groupings you need.

### Catcher and First Baseman Drills

You will need at least two catchers. Ask the players what positions they played before and what position they would like to try. You need a kid who *wants* to play catcher, then you will have to press one or two into duty as a backup. Find a tough kid who fits the catcher description in chapter five. A tall lefty is great at first base, but more important, he must be able to catch throws from infielders.

1. Stance. Go over the fundamentals of the catcher's crouch and the first baseman's stance and stretch. Have the player demonstrate form. Look at each aspect: feet, torso, both hands, balance, position near the batter. The tuck of a catcher is reminiscent of a downhill skier. Use the checklist.

2. Wild thing drill. Catcher in full gear behind the plate. First baseman alternates with catcher (she should also wear a mask and shin guard). Coach throws ball, initially a rubber-coated hard ball, high, low into the dirt, inside and out. The idea is to get the catcher and first baseman to practice handling wild throws and throws in the dirt. They will see plenty during a game and need to be able to stop these throws. A player or parent can throw the errant balls, just make sure someone is picked who can place the ball at difficult but catchable spots. Not too hard at first!

3. Pop-up drill. The coach stands at the plate and lobs the ball, with backspin, straight up in the air. The catcher springs from the crouch to locate and catch the ball. Throw it into foul territory so the first baseman and catcher can work out calling for the ball. Remember, the first baseman should have priority since he has a bigger glove.

4. Bunt drill. The ball is bunted down the first baseline, and the catcher scrambles from a crouch to scoop it up (two hands) and throw to first. Step to the infield side of the line to ensure the ball doesn't hit the runner.

### Catcher-Pitcher-Shortstop Drills

1. Steal drill. Catcher practices throwing the ball to second and third bases. The idea is to speed up the transition of the ball from the glove to the throw. Catchers won't get much action on this play until kids are allowed to steal on regulation fields. Nonetheless, it should be practiced.

2. Passed ball drill. Most steals are on passed balls. The catcher should practice hustling to the ball, snatching it up and preparing to throw. Have a kid on first base run to second as the ball hits the backstop. (See figure 6-2.) Work with the catcher on the optimum times to throw and not to throw. It's important for the catcher to know when she has a chance to get the runner out and just as important to know when there is no chance and a throw only risks another error. The catcher has only a split second to decide, as she glimpses the runner's position, and it is a situation that must be practiced. Even more important is the drill when a runner is on third. See chapter five for details on snatching the ball to the pitcher covering the plate. (See figure 6-2.)

### Infielder Drills

1. Outahere drill. All infielders line up and take turns straddling a bag, preparing to tag a runner out. Place a loose bag on a long strip of cardboard. Have a coach throw to the fielder as runners slide into the tag. Have another coach stand on the cardboard so it doesn't slide. Tell the kids to slide into the bag and avoid their teammate's feet. (See figure 6-2.)

2. Machine gun drill. Stand midway between the plate and the pitcher's mound, and fire grounders at one fielder. As soon as the fielder releases a throw back to your catcher, fire another at the same player. Speed it up as fast as that player can take it, then go on to another player.

3. Pepper. A fun drill for all players. A coach takes two infielders, side by side about 10 feet or less from the coach. The coach hits grounders and the infielders throw the ball back, low, directly to the bat for another grounder. This improves reflexes. (See figure 6-2.)

4. Fungo drills. The bread-and-butter practice for infielders. One coach or parent hits grounders from the plate to infielders in their

regular positions. He also hits shallow pop-ups to the infield. In-fielders practice throwing to all bases, including home. After ten minutes, switch the kids to give the backup players a shot at positions they will play.

5. Lob drill. This drill should use the first baseman and pitcher for first base lobs and the shortstop and second baseman for second base lobs. With players in position, hit a grounder to the first base-man. He lobs the ball to the pitcher, who runs to cover first. Also do grounders between short and second, so they can lob to each other.

6. Rundown drills. All infielders, pitchers and catchers. Use different groups for different bases. Remember each baseman must be backed up. (See chapter three.)

i) Catcher, pitcher, third base, shortstop. Rundown between third and home. Instruct the first and second basemen to cover their bags. Left fielder backs up third.

ii) Pitcher, third base, shortstop, second base. Rundown between third base and second base. Catcher and first baseman cover their bases.

iii) Shortstop, second base, first base, pitcher. Rundown between second base and first base. Catcher and third baseman cover their bases.

### Outfielder Drills

1. Fungo drill. Again, the bread-and-butter practice for outfield-ers. Hit pop-ups, liners and hard grounders. It might work better to throw the pop-ups (if your arm can take it). Have one player in close to relay the ball. At young ages, use a soft ball.

### Batting Practice

Most of your practice time is needed for batting practice. It takes an hour or more to give each kid a lot of quality time. It's critical to have a coach or parent who can get the ball over the plate consis-tently with some speed. Fortunately, I could always do it, and I pitched to the younger kids while down on one knee so the ball would come in level to the batters. Don't underestimate the impor-tance of this. Find someone else if you don't have the control. (Don't burn out your pitcher's arm!)

1. Twenty-and-out drill. Give each kid fifteen to twenty pitches. Then get each one up again. It's better than having each kid try thirty to forty at once. Throw the ball so the batter can hit it. Throw harder for the better batters. The idea is to start easy and finish stronger. If a kid has trouble, move in as far as needed to get him to make contact, then slowly move back. Don't use a catcher—that will just slow things down, and the catcher will wear out. Use a bucket of ten to fifteen balls. Have a player or another parent with you on the mound to help receive the balls from fielders. Keep up a good pace. Tell fielders to hold the ball for a few pitches, so you can pitch several in a series without interruption. Make sure your infielders are focused on the batter for each pitch. The idea is to keep a good pace but not take chances with too many balls flying about.

2. Switch-hit drill. I always have my players take five or so pitches batting lefty, or righty if they are a lefty. Switch hitting is more important later on, perhaps by college, when pitches come in a lot faster, because the switch helps a batter see the ball. A lefty batter can see the ball better from a righty pitcher. The ball approaches the plate from more in front of the batter rather than from the side or behind. However, it's also good for young kids to switch because it gives them a different perspective. I believe it helps train them to look more closely at the ball, and their swing is less "automatic" when they have to concentrate more.

3. No-pitch drill. In this drill the coach or parent lobs the ball from a spot about 5 feet from a plate, off to the side of the batter. (See figure 6-2.) The batter faces a link fence or a net to stop the ball. I once used a clothesline and a heavy blanket to stop the ball. The batter tries to hit the ball dead center, looking at the spot on the ball. A goal is to have the ball hit the net or screen waist to shoulder high—you want line drives! This is a good drill to increase the amount of batting practice without using the field.

### Pitchers

The key to pitching is proper form. Study the form fundamentals in chapter five, and watch your pitchers in practice. Get the pitchers in a group at each practice. You can do it off to the side for what I call a *sideline pitch* drill. Have the catcher or a parent catch. Get

FIGURE 6-2

## POPULAR DRILLS

Passed Ball Drill. Pitcher runs from mound and straddles plate, catcher runs to backstop and snatches ball to pitcher. Have a base runner so timing can be practiced.

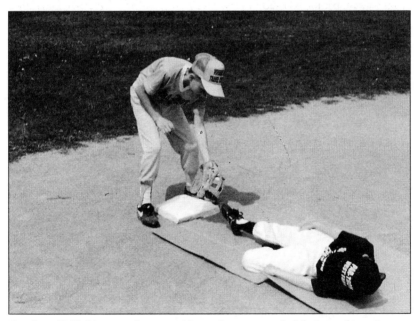

Outahere Drill. Line up players and have them run and slide into a base. I use cardboard to cushion the slide and avoid abrasions. Fielder must bend knees more to avoid missing tag.

FIGURE 6-2 (cont.)
# POPULAR DRILLS

Pepper. Line up several infielders. Tap out grounders. Have player toss ball back directly to the bat for next tap.

No Pitch Drill. Lob ball from the side, about 5 or 6 feet from batter. Batter hits ball into net or screen, a few feet away to the left (not in picture). Great drill to conserve field space.

something to use for a pitcher's rubber, and something for a home plate. Don't try to change too much at once. One thing at a time is best. Have the pitcher look at pictures of the six parts of proper pitching form: address, windup, crane, kick, delivery and follow-through. Talk about the grip and opening the hips.

Throw easy while working on form. Use videotape as available. Form practice for pitchers is essential. Have the pitchers learn control by the *hitting the corners* drill, high and outside, high and tight, low and inside, low and away. Go around the four corners three or four times, take a break and do it again.

## Work on Team Execution

The last half hour of practice is a good time to get the whole team together for drills that require a full set of fielders and base runners. For these drills, players should be in their regular positions.

1. Cutoff drills. Start with bases empty, then add runners to first, then first and second, then bases loaded. Hit the ball to any fielder, infield or out. Get the kids into the habit of thinking ahead of time where they will go with the ball. Talk about their choice and execution after each play. The idea is to run through each cutoff play for each outfielder, but pepper a few grounders at infielders to keep them on their toes. If the ball gets through, then the cutoff play is made. Play live conditions: rundowns, slides (if the field is not too rough), tag outs.

2. Scrimmage. There is usually not enough time to play a game, but if you organize the practice well enough you can sometimes get a few innings in. I divide up the kids and parents. Parents play the outfield and bat lefty or one handed if they are good hitters. (Usually I just use parents as steady defense, but some want to take a few swings too.) I usually pitch to make sure that the ball gets over and is hittable.

3. Signals. The *stay or go* drill is designed to work runners with the third base coach. Line up the team midway to third base and let them come one at a time. Give one of the four signs to stay, slide, turn the corner or go home (see chapter four). Another good drill halfway through practice is *signals says*. Gather the team around you, and go over the signs. Give them a key sign and go

through a series of signs. The first one to get the sign yells it out and goes for a water break. Continue until half the team gets a break, then give the remaining players fifteen push-ups.

## Motivate, Communicate, Lead

This is such an important topic that I devoted much of chapter seven to it—both parents and coaches should be sure to read that chapter.

Two keys to motivating, communicating and leading are to stay positive and to reward good effort. When you need to correct a player, remember that it's actually the *effort* you're trying to improve. Don't attack the kid personally. Yelling to motivate players can be great, but don't cross the line to humiliating them.

## THE PRACTICE PLAN

Each practice should have a written practice plan. It just takes a few minutes to think through what you want to accomplish, and it does wonders for efficient use of time to hit the practice running. I've developed a form that can be found on the last page of this chapter. Make a few dozen copies of it. You can waste a lot of practice time if you are not organized, and you can triple the value of the practice if you are.

Practice plans vary over the course of a season. The focus of the first weeks of practice, usually starting in April for grade-school level play, is (1) batting practice, (2) figuring what positions should be assigned to each player and (3) conditioning. Then focus shifts to individual skills, and only then to team dynamics. Note that I said the *focus* changes—all of these concepts are involved in every week's practice all year.

The following are typical sample practice plans for different weeks into the season. I start at 5:30 on weekdays, since coaches at grade-school levels have day jobs. In April you may get light until 7:30. A Saturday practice usually lasts two and a half hours.

## Early April Practice Plan

TIME     ACTIVITY

Earlybirds  Run a lap, have a catch to warm up the arm.

5:30 P.M.   **CONDITIONING:** Quick cali set, leg stretch set.

| | |
|---|---|
| | **SPEED DRILLS:** Robot, bounce, buttkick, goosestep. |
| | **AGILITY DRILLS:** Simon says, carioca. |
| 5:50 P.M. | Call team together. Brief comments. |
| 6:00 P.M. | **BATTING PRACTICE:** Coach pitches twenty-and-out. Six fielders (three outfield, three infield), one player on deck to retrieve balls for the pitcher and one batter. |
| | **PITCHING PRACTICE:** Sideline pitch drill with coach or other pitchers catching. Four pitchers. Go thirty minutes two pitching, two catching. Then send group for batting practice and try out four more pitchers. After a few practices, stay with the four best. |
| | **SPECIALTY DRILL:** If you have the coaching help, take a few prospective catchers, first basemen or infielders and work on specialty drills such as stance, wild thing, pop-up, outahere. A vision therapy drill such as the Brock string or rotations is always a good sideline drill. These can wait a few weeks if you are pressed. |
| 6:30 P.M. | **WATERBREAK:** Continue. |
| 7:00 P.M. | **DEFENSIVE PRACTICE:** Fungo to infield and outfield. Use two coaches, one hitting grounders to infielders and one, off to the side, hitting to outfielders. Evaluate defensive potential of each player. Infielders make the throw to first base. Watch for too much throwing, so after a while have them just field the ball and lob it home. Rotate players around the horn and into outfield. |
| 7:25 P.M. | **WIND SPRINTS.** |
| 7:30 P.M. | **CLOSING COMMENTS, PRACTICE OVER.** |

## Mid- to late April Practice: A Saturday

| TIME | ACTIVITY |
|---|---|
| Earlybirds | Run a lap, have a catch to warm up the arm. |
| 11:00 A.M. | **CONDITIONING:** Do quick cali set, leg stretch set. |
| | **SPEED DRILLS:** robot, bounce, buttkick, goosestep. |
| | **AGILITY DRILLS:** Simon says, carioca. |
| 11:20 A.M. | Call team together. Brief comments. |
| 11:30 A.M. | **BATTING PRACTICE:** Coach pitches twenty-and-out. Six fielders (three outfield, three infield), one player on deck to retrieve balls for the pitcher, and one batter. |
| | **PITCHING PRACTICE:** Sideline pitch drill with coach or other pitchers catching. Do hitting corners drill. Four pitchers. Go thirty minutes two pitching, two catching. Then send group for batting practice. |

**SPECIALTY DRILLS:** As with earlier practice plan, if there is help, do drills that can conveniently be done on a sideline, such as stance, wild thing, pop-up, outahere. Introduce signs and signals drills.

12:00 P.M.  **WATER BREAK:** Continue.

12:30 P.M.  **DEFENSIVE PRACTICE:** Fungo to infield and outfield. Use two coaches, one hitting grounders to infielders and one, off to the side, hitting to outfielders. Incorporate double-plays, machine gun drill, run-down drill, lob drill, bunt, steal and passed ball drills. What you don't get in in one practice, do the next time.

**BATTING PRACTICE:** Have a coach take a couple of players at a time for the no-pitch drill.

1:00 P.M.  **WHOLE TEAM PRACTICE. CUTOFF DRILLS.**

1:25 P.M.  **WIND SPRINTS.**

1:30 P.M.  **CLOSING COMMENTS, PRACTICE OVER.**

## May Practice: A Weekday

TIME          ACTIVITY

Earlybirds   Run a lap, have a catch to warm up the arm.

5:30 P.M.  **CONDITIONING:** Do quick cali set, leg stretch set.

**SPEED DRILLS:** Robot, bounce, buttkick, goosestep.

**AGILITY DRILLS:** Simon says, carioca.

5:50 P.M.  Call team together. Brief comments.

6:00 P.M.  **DEFENSIVE PRACTICE:** Fungo to infield and outfield for 10 minutes. Practice slides, wild thing, steals, passed balls, machine gun. Go for 10 minutes each drill.

**BATTING PRACTICE:** No-pitch drill, as players become available.

7:00 P.M.  **SCRIMMAGE GAME:** Live pitching, balls and strikes. Move very quickly to save time (on deck batter jumps in, players run on and off, pitchers warm up quickly, use several balls, etc.). However, stop play and discuss wrong plays. Use signs and signals.

7:50 P.M.  **WIND SPRINTS.**

8:00 P.M.  **CLOSING COMMENTS, PRACTICE OVER.**

These plans work well for most age groups. At younger ages, you can shorten the conditioning a bit and spend some time talking baseball. Get the kids in a circle and ask them questions: What's a steal? What's a ball? What's a strike? Who can name the fielding positions? What's a triple, a homer, a double, a single?

Get them all around home plate and demonstrate proper stance and swing form. Tell them about bad form. Demonstrate defensive form. Spend a fair amount of time on this each practice until they have it right. For younger kids it will take longer and be less productive to spend time on specialty drills, but make sure you acquaint the players with every concept and do some drills. Of course, they need a lot of time batting and fielding.

One final word about specialty drills and using parents. I once had ten parents, men and women, on the field helping out. I set up what we called stations, simultaneous drills on separate areas of the field. Here is what it looked like.

1. Twenty-and-out drill. One parent pitching on one knee, and three parents in the outfield shagging balls. Two players, one batting and one picking up balls.

2. Two no-pitch drill stations at the outside of the backstop at either end. Two parents and two batters.

3. Pepper drill. One parent, two fielders, in foul territory.

4. Form drill for pitchers. Two pitchers throwing to each other or to a parent.

5. Outfield pop-ups. I had two fielders and a parent in foul area who threw pop-ups to the fielders.

6. Form corner. Two players. Whatever their position they worked with a parent on form.

That's it. I had twelve players at practice. I rotated them from station to station, ten minutes a station, an hour for the whole deal. If I had two more kids and a parent, I would have done some vision therapy drills also (see chapter eight). The kids at such a practice get the equivalent experience of six practices where coaches only do one thing at a time.

# DAILY PRACTICE SCHEDULE

## DAY_____

TIME          ACTIVITY

_____        _____

_____        _____

_____        _____

_____        _____

_____        _____

_____        _____

_____        _____

_____        _____

_____        _____

_____        _____

_____        _____

_____        _____

NOTES _____

_____

_____

_____

_____

# Chapter Seven

# THE PSYCHOLOGY OF COACHING BASEBALL

## JUST A GAME?

Aren't kids too young to learn all this? Will the competition, the stress on winning, be too much at certain ages or for certain types of kids? How do you motivate a rambunctious ten-year-old? How do you get kids to play with consistency? What is a good age?

If your players, or your son or daughter, are very young, then it will be a few years before the more technical parts of the game will be understood well enough to routinely occur on the field. But all of it—including the more complicated concepts of throwing ahead of the lead runner and the cutoff—all of it should be taught at all ages. Don't underestimate your players; some of them will grasp these concepts. The basics, especially hitting basics, should be emphasized right away before bad habits form. I pitched to my kids as soon as they could hold a bat, and I insisted they employ proper form. (Remember Keith, the potential all-star who lost two years because of his nearly incurable habit of dropping his right side?)

A lot of the refinements such as the cutoff concept, backing up positions and the rundown technique take time and maturity. I had a group of ten-year-old all-stars one year, and I started to drill them on more advanced cutoff concepts. I knew they would actually use little of it for a long time, but they had never even been exposed to it and had to start sometime. Maybe if parents and coaches set the stage in the early years, some of the advanced concepts will click by age ten. But if your players are green, don't worry about it, concentrate on the basics, cover the advanced stuff, but don't expect too much too soon.

Believe me when I say there is no magic age for starting baseball. Look at the age of kids mastering moves in gymnastics, soccer and other sports at seven and eight years old. It's not that younger kids can't learn. They just need someone who understands refined concepts and has the time and ability to teach them. A lot depends on how much time you have to practice, and, unfortunately, weather and field availability are usually problems.

There isn't anything in this book that's over the heads of young kids. Just start somewhere, and the kids will absorb as much as you have the time and patience to teach them. Some skills will take a few sessions, some require much more, some will take years, but it will happen. Like learning how to whistle, suddenly one day it's there, and you sense it was always really simple to do.

As to stresses and motivation, read on!

## ON WINNING

*Our society is ferociously competitive in spirit. Pressuring children too hard may turn them into adults so obsessed with being first that they get no joy out of life except in the narrow field of competition. They neither give nor get pleasure in their relationships with spouses, children, friends, and fellow workers.*

Dr. Benjamin Spock

*The main idea is to win!*

John McGraw, Manager, New York Giants, 1899-1932

Feelings on the importance of winning run strong. As with religion and politics, everyone thinks they are right. Vince Lombardi, the legendary Green Bay Packer football coach, once said, "Winning isn't everything . . . it's the only thing." Others say if you are going to keep a score you should try to win.

Let's face it, if you tell kids winning is no big deal, they may nod, but they are not really buying it. They *know* about winning. They know the kids on the other team will gloat and taunt them back at school. They know about trophies and news articles. They hear the empty silence after a loss.

Well, the truth of it is somewhere in the middle. Kids talk about winning, but I believe that down deep they care even more about how well they are personally doing. I remember one year in my playing days when I was in a terrible slump. The team was winning, but was that satisfactory to me? No way—I was playing lousy. Another year we lost a championship game, but I hit a home run. How did I feel? You guessed it. Sure I wanted to win, but the homer went a long way toward easing the pain.

All right, winning is important in the pros. And maybe it becomes important even for some kids in high school, where scholarship money rarely looks at anybody on a team with a 3-26 record. But in Little League, it's just not as important. Parents and coaches may think it is, but the kids often forget the game and certainly the score as soon as they hit the nearest pool.

What they will remember is how they felt about themselves and how you reacted. Practical advice? I tell my kids something they can believe—that winning is never important in Little League, but that it is always fun to win. That's the truth. They can relate to it. I tell them what's important is how they handle victory or defeat. It's important to try to be as good as they can be, to help each other, and to try to do their best. We surely try to win, but all we can really control is how hard we try.

The field of play stirs up some powerful emotions. It's said that winning builds character, while losing reveals it. Competitive fire can quickly melt an otherwise cool, calm, collected attitude. At the heart of how good a coach or parent you will be is how well you balance *your* need to win with the need to develop healthy young people. This balance will affect your every action, your relationship with each player, and the atmosphere on the field, and it will characterize the memory of your coaching experience for many years to come. Striking that balance involves a continuing struggle between the passions fired up by competition on the one hand and the caring you feel for your players as a responsible adult on the other.

I often find that balance in light of how much talent I have on a team. When I see that we have little chance of winning it all, then I choose to emphasize individual goals. Let's face it, if you can't get there, there is absolutely no sense in getting everyone crazy. But when you have a potential championship team . . . that's the real test!

The key is *balance.* Winning and development both are part of the game. For instance, we all worry about the total dedication required of young Olympic athletes who have sacrificed much of their youth for their quest. Yet we know they have enjoyed moments of glory that seem to transcend life itself, achieving heights most of us only dream about.

It's just not realistic and certainly not helpful to have "experts" like Alfie Kohn tell us in his book *No Contest: The Case Against Competition* (Houghton Mifflin, 1986) that analysis of years of psychological research proves that "competition is poison." That is like telling us not to breathe because the air is somewhat polluted! Competition is a part of life, period! Nor do I think the proper balance was found by such as Eric Margenau, a renowned sports psychologist who suggested in his *Sports Without Pressure* (Gardner Press, 1990) that "Competition is fine, but should be kept friendly . . . Parents should not pressure a child to excel *regardless of that child's abilities* (emphasis added)." I disagree. We all know kids who could excel, but did not do so. They just needed a good push to get going.

Obviously, competition can be taken to extremes. Many of us will remember the ugly scene on national TV when competitive fire drove Ohio State coaching legend Woody Hayes to assault an opposing Clemson player on the field. And we cringed when young tennis star Mary Pierce, symbolic of many troubled young athletes, had to obtain a restraining order against her father from pressuring her. The frenzy to win, riding on the dark horse of fear of failure, can and does get both crazy and destructive!

The issue of competition goes to the essence of the human condition. It is part of our evolution. The answers are complex and most elusive. What is clear to me after many years of coaching and playing sports is that the answer is not to give up.

I recently read in *The New York Times* that some schools are abandoning competitive interaction in their phys ed programs to avoid damaging the feelings of kids who are not outstanding. Isn't it better for kids to learn about and prepare for success and failure in a controlled setting, inside the relatively harmless gymnasium, than in the crucible of adult life? Should we abandon competition, and with it the struggle to succeed, just because we haven't figured out how, as a society, to always do it right? We couldn't quit if we wanted to. It's part of life and we just need to continue to work to find the best balance.

Winning and growth do share common ground. Coaches who

win consistently often are remembered by their former players more for the great lessons of life than for the gold cup on the mantel. They know that the key to success is in knowing how to motivate athletes to win the personal struggle to do their best, to improve beyond their limits, spurred on by their team's goals. They know that the spirit, the will to win, and the will to excel transcend the game itself.

How you resolve the balance between winning and individual development is up to you. If you just recognize the need to strike a balance you are off to a good start.

My own approach in coaching is probably best characterized as a back-and-forth struggle around that balance. When I find myself too focused on the win I step back a bit. I remind myself that while we're going for it, we need to stay on the high road. Every coach has felt that gut wrenching that can stay with you for hours after a game. I think it's enough to be honest about the reality of competitive passion, and then commit ourselves as coaches to doing what we expect of our players, doing our best with it! I believe most coaches want to try to build character and a positive experience for each player, while trying to win the game.

Some coaches never really challenge their teams for fear of upsetting the kids, and these "nice guys" don't do much damage. Of course their players may never make it to the next level of play. Other coaches, at the opposite extreme, feel compelled to win at any cost, and the cost can be tragic for the fragile psyche of a young boy or girl. Find the middle ground. If you find you can't deal with the pressure, then consider whether coaching is right for you and for the kids.

One practical way to get a "reality check" is to pick out a parent who seems to know the other parents well, and ask her how things seem to be going. Parents talk to each other about how they feel and how their kids are feeling, and you can learn things a parent would never tell you directly.

Of course, the issues vary with the age of your team. At preteen levels, the emphasis is always heavily on developing the individual. This doesn't mean that winning is not an issue, it's just not at all important. The focus is solely on development. This is why most programs require that all kids play a certain amount of time. By the time of high school varsity play, the balance is more even. It should never get further than that, but the reality of major collegiate play is that losing coaches don't last.

## ON MOTIVATION

*Rock, I know I'm going to die. I'm not afraid. But someday, Rock, when things on the field are going against us, tell the boys, Rock, to go out there and win just one for the Gipper. Now, I don't know where I'll be then, coach. But I'll know about it, and I'll be happy.*
George Gipp

OK, it's a football story, but it's the best motivation story there is. Legendary Notre Dame coach Knute Rockne waited eight years until, during halftime in a big game against Army, he repeated these last words of his dying quarterback in what was to become the epitome of halftime motivation.

It's a beautiful story, but coaches need to rely on a lot more than speeches to motivate their team. Sure, some coaches have that charismatic quality and can motivate a team just by the sheer strength of their personality. Old Giant manager John McGraw and the more contemporary Yankee Billy Martin were the models of the "hero" coach. However, the rest of us mere "mortal" coaches need to consider motivational techniques that can help us get the job done.

The "secrets" to good motivation are easily found in the growing science of sports psychology. Once considered mere gobbledygook, the mental aspect of competition is now a cornerstone of athletic development at the highest levels of amateur and professional sports. Many teams, including the U.S. Olympic program, employ full-time sports psychologists.

It is not the purpose of this book to go in great depth into the psychology of sports. You will find aspects of psychology spread throughout this book and also in my books on coaching other youth sports such as basketball, football and soccer. I have used psychological insight throughout my twenty years of coaching, and you will probably agree that much of this is common sense that is obvious to any caring adult. The first chapter of this book quickly focused on confidence building and on the right mental approach to the game. My checklist approach to teaching correct form is consistent with the mental checklist urged for athletes by sports psychologists.

If you want to focus more deeply on this area, one of the best books I've read on the subject is *The Athlete's Guide to Sports Psychology: Mental Skills for Physical People* by Dorothy V. Harris and Bette L. Harris (Leisure Press, 1984). I will, however, discuss some emerging motivational techniques that seem to work best.

## Attaboy!

There never will be a better tool than frequent positive reinforcement for young athletes. This is especially true for baseball where there are so many more strikes and outs than hits for a young athlete. It is essential to liberally give out some attaboys (or attagirls!) for good effort. In *Kidsports: A Survival Guide for Parents* (Addison-Wesley, 1983), Dr. Nathan J. Smith, a consultant for the American Board of Pediatrics, reported on his study of two groups of coaches. He found that "the single most important difference in our research between coaches to whom young athletes respond most favorably and those to whom they respond least favorably was the frequency with which coaches reinforce and reward desirable behavior." A pat on the back, a smile, clapping, praise, a wink and a nod, as well as tangible rewards such as mention in a newspaper article, more playing time—all go a very long way toward motivating high performance. I would add that the rewards are even more effective when they emphasize outstanding effort as opposed to a great result. An athlete has complete control over the amount of effort he puts into his game, but the result depends on many things, many of which are beyond the individual's control. Even corrective action, pointing out mistakes, should be sandwiched somehow within some positive comments, such as "Good try, Jack, next time keep your eye on the ball, you can do it!"

Coaches spend a lot of time hollering, trying to motivate players, trying to get them to increase their energy level, and to develop that all important desire to perform. However, there is a line that shouldn't be crossed—humiliating a player. The idea is to be firm, to let players know that they can do better if they reach deeper into their gut. I like to ask players if they gave it their best shot. "Was that your best effort?" "Is that all you have to give?" "Don't you have more 'pop' than that in your bat?"

Let a player know what you think about his *effort*, not *himself*. Don't personalize it. The kid is a decent person, it's the effort you want more of, so focus on the effort during practice. A kid can relate to trying harder; but he can't relate positively to your telling him he stinks. Explain the problem with fundamentals or form so that he *understands the concept*. Work with him until he gets the idea.

Most important, reward good effort openly and liberally. Praise a good catch. Recognize hustle. Yell out, "That's baseball!" It can get infectious, with all players trying to hear and praise the sound of good bat contact.

Having one set of standards for everyone doesn't mean you shouldn't handle players differently. Some kids respond well when you correct them in front of their peers, others are devasted when you get on them. These kids need to be taken aside so you can sit down with them, find out what's going on in their lives, and see if you can learn what the problem is.

## We Are Family!

I've read the autobiographies of many great coaches. One constant in all of their stories is their ability to relate to the different individuals on their team, to create a family-type environment.

Each kid is different, whether on a team or in a family, and each one needs a personal approach. Most important, even the lowest substitute should be treated with equal respect to the best players. I start each season with a team discussion on what it means to be on a team. One thing I tell the players is that for the rest of the season they are all friends. They are all in a special relationship with each other. I tell them they should say hello in the school hallways, and help each other out, off the field, if needed. I never tolerate criticism of a teammate on the field and quickly bench any offender. I expect kids to urge each other on, to quickly tell a teammate to put a mistake behind him. I promote team dinners and outings and move to break up cliques.

Team building is a proven ticket to success. The concept is widely used in all walks of life and is a staple of Japanese and American business organization. Team building doesn't just happen because

## MOTIVATIONAL PHRASES

| HITTING | FIELDING | AFTER A BAD PLAY AT BAT |
|---|---|---|
| Ya gotta believe | Run it down | Learn from it |
| You're a hitter | Get under it | Shake it off, get the next one |
| Swing a hard bat | Shoot the guy | |
| Swing with confidence | Nothing past you | We'll get it back |
| | Want the ball | Get a better pitch |
| Smack a good pitch | Everything | Good cut, see the ball better |
| You can hit this guy | | Your turn next time |

| AFTER A LOSS | AFTER A WIN |
|---|---|
| Was it your best effort? | It was a team win |
| Let's concentrate more | Super effort |
| How much do you want it? | It's happening |
| We got to swing more | That's baseball |
| We need to run smarter | You earned it |
| We're better than this | Don't gloat, just smile |
| Let's focus more next time | |

a bunch of kids are on a team. It happens because coaches work at it. It's actually quite easy to get done. Just put it in the practice plan, talk to your assistant coaches about it, and opportunities to promote *teamness* will present themselves in abundance.

## Set Goals

To give kids proper motivation you must set realistic goals for the team and for each individual. With specific goals, a kid has something clear and achievable to work on, something to set her sights on. She is not responsible for the whole team or for winning or losing. She is not overwhelmed and defeated by unrealistic expectations. Goals provide stimulation.

I think it's a good idea to have each player set his own goals under guidance of the coach. I usually offer the players a number of categories in which a few goals should be set. One category is conditioning. The goals may be to double the number of push-ups they can do, knock a number of seconds off a 440 sprint or a mile and increase their chin-ups. Other goals relate to specific skills for their position. It may be to improve form of the swing or fielding position. Still other goals relate to game performance, such as number of hits. I might also suggest to a player that he increase his self-confidence, his self-control, his relationship with certain teammates, or his effort at practice. I'll have this written down by the player, and we'll occasionally review progress. Don't set too many goals; just focus on key areas.

Sports are about kids becoming solid adult citizens. Most of them will never make cuts at the high school level; a few may play in college. You will probably never coach a future pro baseball player. It is doubtful that your players will remember much about a specific season twenty years later, certainly not the scores of various games. But I guarantee you one thing. They will remember you for the rest of their lives. The memory of my coaches is etched clearly in my mind. I remember them vividly, for good or for bad. You will not remember all of the kids you coached, particularly if you do it for a number of years, but every one of them will remember you. How do you want to be remembered?

The relationship between a coach and a player is a powerful one. You are not only a parent figure, but you are the final authority in what is, in a player's mind, the most important thing in life. In their athletic experiences kids are finding out things about themselves, for good or bad, and they will always associate those things with their coaches. I always viewed coaching as an awesome responsibility. You may want to ignore the larger picture, but sticking your head in the sand does not change what's really going on. There are many tools you can use to help you make the experience a good one, whether you win or lose as a team, but in the final analysis it comes down to whether you really give a darn enough to accept the larger role of being both a coach and a friend.

## ON PEAK PERFORMANCE

The bane of coaches is whatever it is that makes a kid play great one day and completely fall apart the next day. A kid gets struck out first time up and winds up walking around in a daze all day.

Another kid makes a good catch, and suddenly starts to terrorize the batter's box. One day the shortstop can't find the first baseman even if they were holding hands, other days his play seems transcendent.

Modern science tells us that how we cope with the stress of a challenge before us is largely mental—it's all upstairs. Mental control begins with the "fight or flight" instinct, that is, the natural impulse that arises in cornered animals to respond to a threat by fighting it or fleeing from it. It is a genetic reaction, inherited by humans from their earliest ancestors. There's not a kid alive who hasn't felt those butterflies in the stomach. This reaction under game conditions can create a panic that distracts concentration and even causes muscle spasms. However, when controlled properly, it can lead the athlete to a "zone" of peak performance.

In its February 14, 1994, issue, *U.S. News and World Report*, in an article entitled "The Inner Game of Winning," reported on the research of Stanford University neurobiologist Robert Sapolsky. He found that the properly controlled response to challenge releases a desirable increase in adrenalin and sugar, producing the sense of "heightened awareness and flow" associated with being in a peak "zone." The negative counterpart of this reaction, which he calls the "fearful" response, produces a bodily cocktail laced with a substance called cortisol that can "not only impair performance, but can also lead over the long run to damage the arteries and liver and lead to depression."

Another interesting study, reported in the August 3, 1992, edition of the same magazine, was entitled "The Mental Edge: The Brain Is the Key to Peak Performance in Sports and in Life." Brian Hatfield of the University of Maryland reported that at moments of peak performance, the brain's left side, the analytic side, erupts in a burst of relaxing alpha waves, indicative of a relaxed trancelike state. This allows the right side of the brain, which controls spatial relations and pattern recognition, to control the body.

OK, what does all of this have to do with kids playing baseball? It helps reduce the inconsistency I noted at the beginning of this section.

The research suggests several steps coaches can take to create or strive for the conditions optimal to peak performance.

Some of this coaches have done for years. The time-honored best way to produce a controlled response to game-day excitement is constant repetition during practice. Much of this book deals with the need to repeatedly practice hitting and fielding, including adherence to proper form. This is so game responses become automatic and can occur even if the player is under stress or too excited.

The studies both also suggest that a ritual-like approach to game day is conducive to a relaxed state of mind. A regular pattern of eating, exercise, dressing and pregame discussion is highly recommended. Try to avoid any surprises or deviations. The preset mental routine should apply right up to each pitch during the game. Encourage players to run through a checklist of form (hands up, eye on the ball, whip the bat through the ball, level). Tell them to mentally image the play, imagine themselves with great form scooping the ball and making a perfect throw. They should do this right up to the release of the pitch. This stuff works! It is well accepted at the highest levels of sport. Tell kids that they need to prepare their minds as well as their bodies if they are to reach their best potential.

Sapolsky notes that premature arousal of adrenalin hours before a game can cause the adrenalin level in the blood to drop after a few hours, even to a point below normal at game time. This leads to sub-par performance and is another reason to have relaxed, stable pregame routines. Many coaches now employ Zen-type meditations in their training programs, providing athletes with methods to cause relaxed states of mind at will.

Sports psychologists have anticipated this research for years in their support for mental imaging of athletic routines. Olympic athletes have been tracing their steps mentally for years. What we have now are clear scientific bases for these approaches. These techniques are useful at all levels of play. They are perhaps most needed at the youngest levels where kids cannot control the anxieties of competition. Relaxed game-day rituals, mental imaging, self-esteem affirmations and mental checklists (such as contained throughout this book) are techniques that can be repeatedly practiced.

## Get an Edge

Many coaches have some concept that they use to focus players on achieving peak performance. I always tell my players to try to get an edge over their opponent. I talk about how evenly matched most good teams usually are, and that the winner will be the one that gets some kind of edge over the opponent. This concept helps me to get kids to accept, for instance, the idea of improving their mental approach—it's one way to get an edge. I tell kids to double the number of push-ups they can do, since the kids on other teams probably aren't doing it. That way they can get a bit stronger than their opponents.

## ON PARENTS

Interfering parents have become a major problem for coaches in most sports. It seems more so for baseball than for some other sports, and that may be because parents are usually closer to the team. In baseball, parents are right on top of the team, so their complaining is more visible. Nonetheless, it is a problem in all sports.

I have no problem with parents who are just trying to communicate to the coach and find out whether there is some problem they need to be aware of. But often parents are argumentative, and sometimes they're downright insulting.

Of course, you don't need to take any gas from a pain in the neck. But before you get too defensive, think about what's going on. Most parents die a little bit when they see their child going through a bad time. Maybe the child is not playing much, having self-doubts, and acting out at home or school because of it. Parents feel the pain along with their kids. It's tough finding out you're not good enough. But hear them out! Give them some ideas that help them understand what the problem is, and perhaps you can focus them on things they can do to help their son or daughter. Tell them you are "on" the kid because you think he can do better, and you are trying to arouse his potential. Maybe you can get some insight into what is troubling a young boy or girl. Maybe, just maybe, you are dead wrong, and you need to give the kid another look. Tell them you will take a look. I've seen kids who sat on the bench as a sub for half a season suddenly come alive and wind up starting the rest of the season.

Most of all, keep in mind that you're talking about their kid! Parents may feel a bit threatened by your control over their child.

As a parent, I have had uneasy feelings about coaches—it's quite natural. A little patience on your part can defuse some strong emotions. You can turn a potential feud into something that helps the child, and ultimately the team. Try it.

On the other hand, parents who abuse their children during a game are a major problem. These are the parents who scorn their children for striking out or missing a catch. It's the worst thing in sports to see. You do not have to put up with this! Talk to such parents and ask them to keep quiet. If they don't, remove them from the field.

One parent threatened me with removing his son as well. My response was merely that I hoped he wouldn't, but that not playing was probably better than what was going on, and that it would not continue under my watch! The parent stayed home; the kid played.

Frankly, as noted earlier, I rarely have problems with parents. When you can achieve a certain level of team spirit, it becomes infectious and negativity gets left behind. I always seek to empower parents, get them involved with the team in some manner: as coaches, as ball shaggers, in charge of water breaks, in charge of fund drives, in charge of uniforms, on phone trees. Delegate as much as possible, and you'll bring parents into the team dynamic. My section on practice plans pointed to ways that parents can help keep more activity going on in practice. Parents who are athletes can pitch batting practice, hit fungoes, even instruct speciality drills. Encourage parents to bring a glove and have a catch with their child before practice to warm up the player's arm. A parent stationed in the outfield can help keep players focused. Parents in foul territory can retrieve balls. Push gently to get them involved; don't push too hard.

## NOTES FOR PARENTS
### How Can I Get My Child Interested in Baseball?
The most important way is by avoiding the negative stuff. If your child is afraid of the ball, fearful of being embarrassed, or tired of your impatience (if you are yelling at her, and getting annoyed or frustrated), she will never be interested. Tell her she is a hitter already, and you are going to work with her to develop it. Communicate. Discuss the things in this book—talk baseball, go to a pro

game or to a local high school game. Watch some baseball on TV, work with your child in trying to collect a whole series of baseball cards. If you go out and coach her and she gets better, you won't have to worry about interest.

One afternoon I got home from work and Joey was on the stoop waiting for me with a ball and two gloves. "Hey, Dad, want to catch a few?" Interest? I can't turn it off. He tells his friends that I'm his buddy, and baseball is one of the main reasons for our friendship. You work closely with your child on something like this, and he will not only be interested in baseball, he'll become interested in you, and you in him. How can you lose?

## Behavior at Games

I'm not going to tell you to just sit there and be quiet. I'm not going to tell you to reduce your energy by one iota. But if you read this book carefully, you know what to do at games. First, don't add any pressure to your child or anyone's children. Second, say intelligent, helpful things like "Keep your eye on the ball," "Keep the elbow up," "On your toes," "Two outs," "You're a hitter,"—things that will help your child remember the basics. See the sidebar on page 123 for good phrases to call out. If your daughter swings and misses, yell "Good cut." Tell her to get a better pitch next time. Be positive.

If a batter strikes out swinging, I always clap my hands. A batter who swings will hit the ball at some point—I want the batter who strikes out swinging to be happy. On the other hand, if a batter takes a called third strike and the ball was over the plate, I don't yell anything. I take the player to the side and we talk about the fact that you can't have fun unless you swing the bat.

Another thing you can do at games is get to know the other parents on your team. It's really a beautiful thing when teams become one big family. Most of mine have been that way, because I promote it as a high priority. It makes everything more loose, more relaxed, and that's better for the kids. It also can lead to some rewarding friendships and to a deeper feeling of community, and that's icing on the cake. In addition, you might get another parent more interested in helping his or her son or daughter, and that's super. Finally, tell other parents to read this book.

# How to Deal With the Coach

I hope you will have read this book and practiced with your child for a few years before you ever meet your child's first coach. Then you can offer your help as an assistant or even sign up for the top job. When kids are six to eight years old, there is not much skill on the field to worry about. It is a good starting place for inexperienced coaches.

If you don't coach, I suggest you find another way to get involved. When the coach calls, offer whatever help you can give. If your job prohibits weekdays, offer to help on weekends. Many coaches will be happy for it. If you run into a coach who doesn't want help, there's not much you can do officially, but you can still work with your child at home.

Just walk up to the coach at practice and ask if you can help. Suggest taking a few kids off to the side to have a catch. You can back up the batters for foul pops or help with outfield practice. You can supply some water for breaks. Offer to help with phone calls. Some parents just like to sit and watch practice. I don't mind, most coaches won't either. Besides, it will help you become aware of areas where your child can use some improvement.

If the coach is a negative person, and you will probably get one for your child at some point, you should let the Little League board know about it. Bad coaches need to be weeded out. They can do a lot of damage.

If your child is playing the minimum, but only the minimum, be fair before you approach the coach. Usually, coaches are out to win, and they do play the best players. Just work a little harder, and your child may improve enough to play more. If the coach is being unfair, then talk to him about it. It is a difficult thing for all involved, so please be sure it's not just your ego complaining. And, for goodness sake, keep your child out of the debate. Kids don't need the negative images involved. Don't get mad—the coach may take it out on your child—but don't duck it either. A few questions to the coach, nicely stated, will help.

*Chapter Eight*

# A SOUND BODY

## VISION

The following will be the most important section in this book for some of your players, maybe for your own child. It reveals what may be the best kept secret in baseball and perhaps in all of sports. It's about vision, eyesight: how critical it is and how to improve it.

As I look back on my nearly two decades of coaching baseball and at my many success stories, I'm also reminded of the many young players who came to the game full of hope and excitement but who just never made it. Others did well enough but, inexplicably, they continually performed below the level I expected for them. Like all kids, they dreamed of those game-winning hits or rally-snuffing catches. They just never seemed to get it done.

Some of these kids were good athletes. They knew they could do better, knew they had it in them, but only could put up average numbers. Some had a miserable season or two and never came back to the game.

Surely, for many it just wasn't there. Their gifts of life were elsewhere, in the laboratory, with music, or in other skills, just not in baseball. That's life! But I have become convinced that for many a substantial part of the problem was merely in their inability to see the ball clearly enough to make solid contact or to judge accurately its distance and speed.

Stories about the importance of eyesight to baseball are legendary. Perhaps the most famous is that of Ted Williams, one of the best pure hitters of all time. He batted .344 lifetime, smacked 521 homers, won two MVPs and two triple crowns, and was the last player to hit over .400! Ted used to say that he could actually see the ball hit the bat. Well, we certainly teach our players to try to do that, but I've never seen a fastball hit my bat and I doubt most people reading this book have either. The colorful former umpire Ron Luciano challenged Ted on it one day. Ted smeared his bat with black pine tar and said he would hit the ball and then indicate whether or not the bat hit the seam on the ball or even whether it touched two seams. Williams got most of them right!

Ted mastered the rapid eye movements known as saccades, which relate to eye-tracking skills. When he was a kid, Ted used to hit bottle caps spun at him by a friend, and I believe this is what improved the rapid eye movements needed to track a baseball.

Babe Ruth was found to have visual acuity far superior to the average player. Moreover, the importance of vision is clear from major league's experience with the introduction of night baseball in the post-World War II era. All agree the ball is harder to see at night; field lights don't equal normal daylight. The result was that the average batting averages tumbled about twenty points! The difference between a .280 batting average and a .260 average will determine whether a player makes it or not in the pros.

I'm not describing major differences in eyesight in this chapter. Just a small subtle difference in visual acuity is enough to lead to enormous differences in how well a batter can hit baseballs.

This fact is not lost on professional baseball players. Vision therapy is a rapidly growing staple of the off-season preparation of major league players. The sports literature reports that many other sports such as golf, tennis, hockey and basketball are including emphasis on visual acuity in training routines.

The June 1992 issue of *Sport* magazine reported on Chicago Cubs assistant general manager Syd Thrift, a long-time innovator in baseball, who introduced visual sensory training to his players. The article stated, "His eye training regimen consists of a series of vision tests, exercises for the fourteen eye muscles and follow-up workouts designed to improve concentration, visual focus, depth perception and hand-eye coordination." Thrift said, "Pitchers perform better since they are more focused on the target. Batters can use two eyes as one, picking up the ball as soon as it leaves the pitcher's hand and quickly identifying the pitch." The article noted that greats such as George Brett, Barry Bonds and Bobby Bonilla benefited from the therapy, and that the best visual acuity tested had been Don Mattingly's.

In an astonishing book, *20/20 Is Not Enough*, Arthur S. Seiderman and Steven E. Marcus revealed new and effective ways to dramatically improve vision. They claimed that 70 percent of Americans have less than adequate vision. Moreover, vision is not fully developed until age ten or eleven. Intensive reading in school, watching television, and working at computer terminals all further reduce visual acuity. So, is it surprising that so many ten-year-olds in Little League don't make good ball contact? What is really frustrating is that the book suggests that most visual disorders go undiagnosed and could easily be treated.

The good news is that vision can be improved. Even if your child has 20/20 vision, this does not mean he cannot improve other aspects of vision such as depth perception, the ability to track clearly a fast-moving object and hand-eye coordination. The difference with only a small amount of therapy can be enormous.

It is not the objective of this book to give medical advice or to go in depth on the biology of the eye itself. The book I mentioned above is available in bookstores or libraries (Knopf, 1989). Other superb books are: *Healthy Eyes, Better Vision* by Jeffrey Anshel (Body Press, 1990); and *Your Eyes!* by Thomas L. D'Alonzo (Avanti Publishing, 1991).

Suffice it to say here that the eyes are like binoculars, and when they don't work well together they get out of focus, resulting in difficulty in seeing things that are close (hyperopia or farsightedness), difficulty in seeing things far away (myopia or nearsightedness), difficulty judging depth or speed of an approaching object, or other ailments.

I advise you to see an eye doctor and have your child's eyes tested. If one of your players seems to have some difficulty seeing the ball, suggest it to the parents. Tell them to read this book, so they can consider whether it would be useful to engage in vision therapy even if there is a more obvious eye disorder.

Vision therapy has advanced far enough that some exercises can safely be done at home. I'll list a few that appear more commonly in the literature and that apply to the skills needed in baseball. Again, the best practice is to first seek a doctor's advice.

## Vision Therapy Drills

1. Brock string. Tie a 4-foot string, with a large knot or black tape marking the center and a point several inches from each end,

FIGURE 8-1
## VISION THERAPY DRILLS

**Brock String.** Improve focusing and depth perception. Move the focus from one marker on the string to another. The line will form a figure X in the middle, and the X will appear more like a V or an A at the end markers. See how this drill, usually done at home, can be practiced on the field.

to an object at eye level while seated. Stretch the line taut and hold against the nose. Looking at the center spot will reveal an X pattern. (See figure 8-1.) The far spot will reveal an A pattern, and the near spot a V pattern. Practice shifting the gaze from spot to spot until it feels smooth and easy to do. Eventually you can shorten the string. Do this for several minutes each day. It will improve focusing and depth perception. This drill can be done at home or at practice. (Check with parents first!)

2. Marsden ball. Get a rubber ball about 4 inches in diameter. Suspend it from overhead to about eye level while seated. Write letters and numbers all over the ball in ink. (They should be clear, dark letters on a light-colored ball.) Cover one eye and tap the ball lightly. Try to call out a letter you see and quickly touch it with your finger. Do each eye for a few minutes. (See figure 8-2.) This improves eye-hand coordination and the ability to track a moving object. If the ball can be affixed securely enough, use a broom handle to bounce it off a wall. Try to maintain a fluid and continuous pace. Use a smaller ball to make it tougher. With parental consent,

the Marsden ball drill can be done at practice. Have one player hold the string for another.

3. Fixation drill. Hang a ring from a string to eye level while standing. Stand a step away with a long pencil. Cover the left eye, step toward the ring with the right foot and, holding the pencil in the right hand, try to put the pencil through the ring without touching it. After a few minutes switch eyes, use the left hand, and step with the left foot. After mastering this drill, try it with a moving target. This drill improves hand-eye coordination. (See figure 8-2.)

4. Rotations. Place a marble in a pie tin or frying pan held about 15 to 18 inches from the eyes. Holding the head still, rotate the marble and try to follow it for a few minutes. Change direction for another two minutes. This improves tracking ability. (See figure 8-2.)

5. Accommodation drill. Doctors use a device called an Accomotrac, based on biofeedback theory, to improve focusing problems, particularly nearsightedness. An exercise you can do is to sit with a newspaper with normal-sized print at just below eye level, as close as possible to the eye, then place another newspaper with large headlines 15 to 20 feet away. Cover one eye. Shift focus back and forth from one to the other. This can also be done with any nearby small object and any distant object.

6. Convergence drills. Place this book on a desk with figure 8-3 at normal reading distance. Hold a pencil between the two sets of circles and slowly move the pencil point toward your eyes. At a point about 6 inches from your eyes, a third circle will appear between the other two. The outer circle should appear closer than the inner one. When it seems clear, shift the eyes to something else and bring them back again to the pencil tip. Do this until the focus remains smooth and clear upon the middle figure. Do it ten times. (See figure 8-3.)

Another convergence drill is to hold the circles up at reading distance but just below eye level. Sit several feet from a wall. Focus on the wall, and the third circle should again appear. This time the small inner circle should appear closer. Close eyes and reopen to the pencil point. Do this several times until the focus stays smooth and clear. After this is mastered, the pencil can be dispensed with, and the distance of the figures can be made a bit closer. You can

FIGURE 8-2

# VISION THERAPY DRILLS

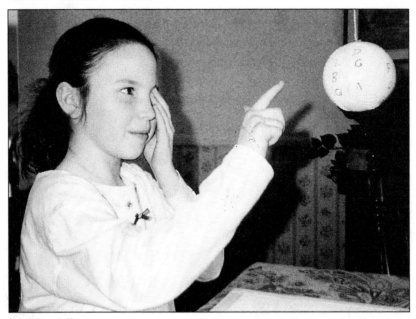

**Marsden Ball.** Improve eye-hand coordination and eye tracking. This drill can also be done on the field with one parent or player holding the string.

**Rotations.** Improves eye tracking ability. Can be done at the field also.

**Fixation Drill.** Improves eye-hand coordination.

FIGURE 8-3

## CONVERGENCE DRILL CONCENTRIC CIRCLES

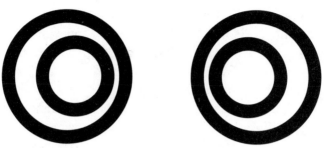

**Convergence Drill.** Set a pencil between the circles and slowly move it toward the nose, staring at the pencil tip. When a third set of circles appears in the background (pencil should be about 6 inches from nose) shift focus from pencil tip to paper, back and forth, not too fast.

also draw the figures on separate cards and separate them more (just a bit, don't strain). Always try to get to a clear focus on the center set of circles.

Teach these drills to your players on a rainy day. Tell them to do them at home. Some can be done at the field. Talk to parents first. Tell parents to get this book and read this section. Your team's vision will improve. Batting and fielding will improve. Hopefully, some of those kids who otherwise wouldn't make it will have some fun with this great game!

One final thought. Do you know which of your eyes is the dominant one? Make a circle with your thumb and index finger, and extend your arm out at eye level. Fix your sight on a small object and close one eye, then open it and close the other. The dominant eye is the one for which the object does not move! Studies show that batters whose dominant eye is the opposite of their batting side (left eye for righty batters, right eye for lefties) hit for higher average. The dominant eye is closer to the pitch.

## CONDITIONING

I rarely recommend weight training for youth sports, and I certainly don't do so for baseball. I'll discuss this more later in this section.

A good calisthenic program is adequate, and a list of exercises was given in the prior chapter. Push-ups are the best exercise since upper body strength is important to all sports. Tell your players to do fifty to one hundred per day. Chin-ups, as many as the player can do, are also quite helpful. Wrist, forearm and shoulder strength are crucial, and any help that you can give here will be immediately and quite noticeably rewarded on the field. I got my son a set of chest expanders, with springs attached to handles, and he used to do them while watching cartoons. The wrist machine mentioned in chapter six is great for home or practice. I always had one in my duffle bag, and the kids used it after they batted. Rowing exercises are also very good to increase strength and stamina. Pitchers especially need forearm and wrist strength to snap the ball.

After the chest come the legs. Wind sprints are the best leg exercise. Partial squats, halfway bending the knee with some extra weight added, are quite good. Don't bend all the way. The long-standing tradition of running up stairs is excellent. If you have a bench, the leg extender apparatus usually attached is also very good. Whenever using weights, focus on strength conditioning. Use low weights with multiple repetitions. High weight just pumps up size and that's not needed, particularly at youth level play.

Muscles are like bubble gum. If you stretch gum quickly it tears or snaps, but if you stretch it slowly it expands nicely. Stretching before practice and games will help prevent muscles from tearing or snapping. No practice of any kind should begin without some slow jogging, some jumping jacks (for the ankles), and some general stretching (for the upper thigh, trunk and neck). Running sideways and backwards or any agility exercises are quite good also.

As noted, I generally believe that weight training should be avoided by grade-school level players and not started until mid-high-school years. Part of the reason is intuitive: A child's body is growing rapidly until then. I am also aware of some studies done in the 1970s that demonstrated that grade-school kids do not gain strength from weight lifting due to lack of male hormones. These studies also suggested that there was significant risk of injury to kids' growth plates, which are the ends of the long bones that account for growth.

A careful study of 354 high-school football players by Dr. William

Risser of the University of Texas Medical School found that weight lifting can cause severe musculoskeletal injuries, usually muscle strains and often in the lower back—7.1 percent of the players reported injury. Injuries occurred when free weights were used in major lifts such as the clean and jerk, the snatch, the squat lift, the dead lift, the power clean and in the bench, incline and overhead presses. Most injuries occurred in the home and were related to poor technique and form, lack of warm-up, and lack of a spotter to assist.

However, I must report that more recent research suggests a different point of view from my own. In the November 1990 issue of *Pediatrics* (Vol. 86, No.5), the American Academy of Pediatrics Committee on Sports Medicine said, "Recent research has shown that short-term programs in which prepubescent [grade school] athletes are trained and supervised by knowledgeable adults can increase strength without significant injury risk." The statement went on to say: " Interscholastic athletic programs in secondary schools are increasingly emphasizing strength training as a conditioning method for participants in male and female sports. The major lifts are often used . . . Strength training in adolescence occasionally produces significant musculoskeletal injury . . . especially during use of the major lifts. Safety requires careful planning of several aspects of a program. This includes devising a program for the intensity, duration, frequency, and rate of progression of weight use, as well as selection of sport-specific exercises appropriate for the physical maturity of the individual. Proper supervision should be provided during training sessions." The committee also addressed the issue of when kids should be allowed to lift maximal amounts of weight, that is, the greatest amount of weight they can successfully lift. They concluded that this should be avoided until kids have passed their period of maximal velocity of height growth. Young people reach that stage *on average* at age fifteen, but the committee also notes that there is "much individual variation." Consequently, based on the contents of this article, the American Academy of Pediatrics recommends that each child's stage of physical maturity be assessed by medical personnel and that the adults planning strength training programs be qualified to develop programs appropriate for varying stages of maturity.

Another excellent article, "Strength Training in Children and Adolescents," (*Pediatric Clinics of North America*, October 1990), was written by Dr. David Webb at the Center for Sportsmedicine, Saint Francis Memorial Hospital, San Francisco, California. He found that most injuries occurred in the home and were unsupervised and that there is not an inordinate risk of injury in weight training if it's properly done. He also reported that strength training can help kids excel in sports and that it can actually *reduce* the incidence of muscle or tendon injuries in sports.

What does this all mean? Knowledgeable trainers can help young athletes gain strength at all levels of play, and weight training will help them do so. Since most kids are urged to do it, those who don't will be at a disadvantage. However, any program should avoid maximal weight lifts until the mid-high-school years.

Be careful; injury can still occur no matter what. Let's face it. Anyone who has ever lifted weights knows that even if you follow a good program, kids have a powerful urge to finish up with some heavy weights to see how much they can lift. If unsupervised, they will go for the max at some point. This is one of the main reasons I frown on the idea. I also resent the idea that we should heighten the competitive pressure of athletics in grade school by creating a need to strength train to "keep up." But the reality is that at the high school level players will need to do weights if they are to be competitive. As a parent you must ensure that they are supervised and that they follow a sound program. A 7 percent injury rate is quite high, so parents must assert controls on this matter.

A player who undertakes a weight training program, as advised above, should have the supervision and advice of a knowledgeable trainer. Parents should ask their doctor if any preexisting health conditions can be aggravated by such training. High blood pressure is one condition that doesn't mix with weights. Any pain should be reported to the trainer. Warm-up and stretching exercises should be done before lifting. Lifting maximal weights or engaging in *ballistic* sudden jerking exercises such as clean and jerk should not be done. Kids should generally use weights that can be done in sets of fifteen repetitions. They should not lift every day, but every other day at the most. All major muscle groups should get some attention to keep development balanced.

In the weight room, baseball players should emphasize shoulder and light leg exercises. Exercises with dumbbells for shoulder, wrist and forearm strength and for strengthening the rotator cuff are useful. I like best the exercise that has the player lying on the bench with a dumbbell in each hand, arms fully extended outward. The player lifts the weights until they touch. It's the type of exercise that strengthens throwing ability. For the legs, work on hamstrings and knee strengthening. Let the trainer explain how to do these and other exercises needed for a balanced program.

## INJURIES

Carefully check the practice fields. Are there stones or other protrusions? Are there any holes, ruts or tracks? (This is how ankles get sprained.) If you see any, let the players know so they can avoid them. Perhaps you can get a few other parents together to fill in any holes or remove any protrusions or other debris.

Finally, is there a trainer or someone qualified in first aid at practice? This is *very* important during early days of practice. Most leagues require coaches to obtain licenses that expose them to first aid techniques, but is there someone who really knows what to do? If not, remember that parents can take a course and become quite knowledgeable. Perhaps you can get a parent to volunteer as a trainer.

I watched a practice game once in which a kid twisted his knee. The coach was shorthanded for players and seemed more concerned about getting the kid back into the game than worrying about the extent of any injury. A few minutes later the kid was back in the action. After a while I noticed he was limping a bit. The coach never looked at him! I told the coach, and the player was removed. As a parent, it pays to attend a few practices to see how sensitive the coach is to injury. A good rule is that a player who complains of any injury to any joint cannot play for at least ten minutes to see if pain or swelling is still present.

No matter how well conditioned a team is, injuries can occur anytime. A common injury is a groin strain, usually caused by sprinting down to first base without warming up. Strained knees, sprained ankles, sore thumbs on the catching hand, and bruised ribs from getting hit by pitches are the most common in baseball. Bloody noses, sprained wrists and forearms, jammed fingers, dislocations and bruises also occur. Thankfully, broken bones are rare, but not rare enough. Most youth baseball teams don't have trained first-aid people, and they should. I went through the program for my son's team, and it was quite good. Ambulances are not usually present at games or at practices, where many injuries occur.

Abrasions often occur on the sides of the legs and elbows, from sliding. These are the most likely cuts to get infected. Wash the wound as soon as possible, with soap if it is handy. Apply a dressing when you can—the sooner the better. Just put some antiseptic on it. If it gets red, pussy or red tracks appear, see a physician.

Lacerations are deeper wounds. Unless bleeding is severe, wash the wound and apply direct pressure with a bandage to stop the bleeding. If the wound is severe or deep, seek first aid. Keep applying pressure, and secure the dressing with a bandage (you can tie the knot right over the wound to reinforce the pressure). Immediately elevate the wound higher than the heart to help slow the bleeding. If the bandage over the wound gets blood-soaked, don't remove it—just apply a new dressing right over it. If the child has lost a lot of blood, you'll need to treat for shock. Keep the player warm with blankets and call for help. If a laceration is major, a butterfly bandage will hold the skin together. Consult a physician immediately for stitches.

Contusions and bruises occur frequently. Apply ice quickly after taking care of any abrasions or lacerations. Ice arrests internal bleeding and prevents or lessens swelling. Ice is the best first aid available for nearly any swelling from bruises or sprains. Apply it very quickly, within minutes, and much internal damage will be spared. Do not move the child, especially if he is down due to a hard collision. He could have a spinal injury, and the slightest movement by an untrained person could do some serious damage.

Sprained ankles, knees or wrists should be immobilized. Apply an ice pack immediately. Act as if there is a fracture until you're sure there is no fracture. Call the ambulance if there is any question in your mind. Get an x-ray to see if there is a break or other damage.

If there is a fracture, immobilize the child completely when possible. There should be no movement at all. Comfort her, get her warm with coats or blankets and get medical help. Do not allow your child to be moved or cared for by anyone who is not medically trained. If she is in the middle of the field during a championship game, the game can wait! Insist on this. Permanent damage can result from aggravating a break.

If a child ever falls to the ground unconscious, see if anyone present has been trained in first aid. The first move, once it is clear that the child will not respond, is to check for the vital signs: airway, breathing and circulation, the ABCs of first aid. Send for an ambulance and let a trained person administer rescue breathing or CPR (cardiopulmonary resuscitation) as necessary. Try to stay calm and let the first-aiders do their job. In all my years of coaching four sports and playing even more, I've never seen CPR needed. I hope that you won't either.

Finally, heat exhaustion can occur during practices or games, particularly late in the season. The body gets clammy and pale. Remove the child from the playing field, apply cool towels and elevate the feet. If the body temperature is very high and pupils are constricted, you should suspect heat stroke. Call an ambulance and cool him down fast. Treat for shock.

Knee injuries are tough. Often the injury will require some sort of arthroscopic surgery to mend cartilage. Modern procedures are quite advanced and simple. Have the child see a knowledgeable sports doctor. Your high school athletic director will know one. Tell your child to play the game safely. Aggressiveness is OK, but players should never intentionally hurt someone. Hope that other parents do the same. I play various sports frequently, and there are often one or two guys who take chances with the health of others. Don't encourage your child to grow up to be like them.

When an injury occurs, insist on rest. I've seen many kids rush back from a sprained ankle, only to have the injury plague them through the years. Don't let it happen! And make sure that your child wears an ankle brace from then on. There are excellent ankle braces on the market today. Get one. The point is that injuries need time to heal right. If you give them that time, the future can have many years of sports for your child. If you don't, it could be over already.

## Serious Injuries

Catastrophic spine or brain injuries among any athletes, especially baseball players, are rare. Yet they happen. I recall just a few years ago a teammate of mine who slid into second base. He dove head-first but then turned his back into the second baseman. As his back hit the fielder's knee, he heard a crack. His back was broken (not badly—he recovered).

There are also cases where kids get hit in the head by a hit or thrown ball. This is obviously a most unpleasant subject, but it is important that you understand some detail. Many deadly injuries of the brain or paralyzing injuries of the spine are caused by earlier blows, sometimes one that occurred a week or more earlier, and a concerned and informed parent can step in and avoid it. A player can receive a concussion, never black out, and that brain swelling then can become lethal days later, triggered by a relatively minor blow.

The point is that *any* level of confusion or headache brought on by a blow to the head should receive *immediate* medical attention. I don't care if it's a championship game—get the player out of the game! The Colorado Medical Society recommends that players who sustain a severe blow to the head be removed for at least twenty minutes and not be allowed to return to the game if any confusion or amnesia persists during that time. A player who loses consciousness should go straight to the hospital.

## THE CARBOHYDRATE DIET

Parents can do only so much to improve their child's athletic ability, but they can do a great deal to maintain his or her good health. All sports require a great deal of energy, and a healthy body goes a long way toward better performance on the field and avoiding injury.

Obviously, a balanced diet is essential. There are many books on diet, and your doctor or school nurse can also advise on the elements of good diet. Good nutrition helps develop strength, endurance and concentration. A good diet balances proteins, carbohydrates and fats. An athlete in training needs mainly complex carbohydrates, about 70 percent of the total diet, with fats (10 percent) and proteins (20 percent) splitting the remainder. Popular today is the food guide pyramid. (See figure 8-4.) Complex carbohydrates dominate the base grouping, reflecting the greater doses of breads, cereal, rice and pasta that are recommended. Vegetables and fruits take up the next level, calling for a few daily servings each. The dairy group and the meat, fish and poultry group are next, with fats last.

Early in the season, an evening meal high in carbohydrates helps maintain energy the next day. Pasta is the best meal for this. A banana each day during this early period helps prevent potassium depletion. Potassium facilitates the process of muscular contraction. Complex carbohydrates are the primary source of fuel and energy for the athlete. They are broken down into glucose, the body's main source of energy. What is not needed is stored for future use. Avoid simple carbohydrates such as sugar and honey. The adage that a candy bar just before a game gives an energy boost is misleading since simple carbohydrates cause unstable supplies of glucose. (Ever notice how tired you feel after a sweets overload?) Good sources of complex carbohydrates are corn on the cob, wild rice, brown rice, whole wheat and whole rye.

## A Typical High-Carbohydrate Diet

### Breakfast
- 8 oz. orange juice or a grapefruit or 8 oz. apple juice
- Bowl shredded wheat (low-fat milk) or oatmeal or cream of farina
- (a) Bacon and two eggs or (b) pancakes and butter
- Several slices of whole wheat toast and butter
- Daily vitamin, adult dosage
- 10 oz. water

### Lunch
- 1 bowl of soup: chicken, clam chowder or vegetable
- 2 pieces broiled chicken or 6 oz. broiled fish
- Green salad with oil and vinegar
- Cooked rice or a potato (no french fries)
- 2 slices of enriched bread
- 12 to 16 oz. milk
- 10 oz. water

FIGURE 8-4

# THE FOOD GUIDE PYRAMID

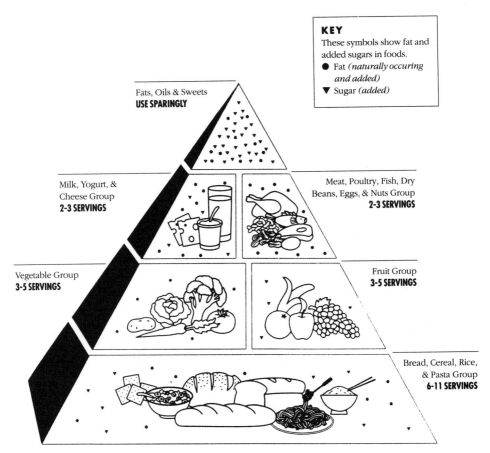

**KEY**
These symbols show fat and added sugars in foods.
● Fat *(naturally occuring and added)*
▼ Sugar *(added)*

Fats, Oils & Sweets
**USE SPARINGLY**

Milk, Yogurt, &
Cheese Group
**2-3 SERVINGS**

Meat, Poultry, Fish, Dry
Beans, Eggs, & Nuts Group
**2-3 SERVINGS**

Vegetable Group
**3-5 SERVINGS**

Fruit Group
**3-5 SERVINGS**

Bread, Cereal, Rice,
& Pasta Group
**6-11 SERVINGS**

The pyramid is an outline of what to eat each day. It's not a rigid prescription, but a general guide that lets you choose a healthful diet that's right for you. The Pyramid calls for eating a variety of foods to get the nutrients you need and at the same time the right amount of calories to maintain a healthy weight.

### Dinner
- 1 bowl of soup: cream of mushroom, cream of potato, or vegetable
- Linguine with tomato or clam sauce
- Baked potato
- Cooked vegetable: corn, broccoli, peas or beans
- Beverage of choice
- 10 oz. water

### Desserts or Snacks
- Bananas, apples, raisins, strawberries, melons
- 10 oz. water

Most teams allow water breaks, so make sure parents know to get their child a water bottle. Midpractice is not a good time to load up on water, so tell the kids to limit themselves to a cup at each break. Kids need a couple of quarts a day, more if it's hot outside late in the season. Drinking plenty of water is a good habit, so be sure they know to drink some at each meal. It is also important to drink plenty of fluids before, during and after practices. Dehydration reduces performance and can lead to serious medical problems.

Alcohol, tobacco and drugs have effects we are all too aware of. What young players may not think about enough is that these substances substantially reduce their playing performance, and reduced performance can put a child out of the running for a starting position, or even for making the team. Be sure to discuss this practical concern.

Sufficient sleep is also a concern. If your son or daughter starts the season with hard sessions of practice, you won't have to worry too much at first, since your child will come right home and hit the pillow. However, into the season, particularly at high school levels, a player may try to burn the candle at both ends. Again, I find that kids relate better when they consider practical consequences of their actions. Lack of sufficient rest diminishes performance. Diminished performance costs playing time.

That's it. That's all I know about coaching baseball. I wish you and your players or your child a happy, healthy and fulfilling relationship, and I wish the kids great fun with a great game. Now, let's play ball!

# Chapter Nine

# CHECKLIST

Now that you have read the book, it's time to get outside and have some fun with your team. I find it useful when I coach to have a checklist of things to remember during practice. For instance, when a boy or girl is batting, I glance at the checklist and it reminds me to focus on different parts of the swing. It also reminds me to keep repeating several things, like "Keep your hands up," "Open your hips with power as you make contact," and "Look at the ball."

So here is a checklist for you to use. Say these things repeatedly.

## HITTING

1. All kids are hitters. Tell them! It will happen with work and confidence. Celebrate improvement of any kind. Be positive.
2. Repetition is essential. They should hit some balls daily or as often as possible. Go to a batting cage. Start slow and build up when ready. Hit a few yourself.
3. Keep your eyes on the ball as it moves from pitcher to the bat. See the whole ball. Watch it spin.
4. Work on the stance. Not too much at once.
   - ✓ Feet as wide apart as the outside of the shoulders.
   - ✓ Stand as deep as allowed in the batter's box.
   - ✓ Rear foot should be back a bit—farther from the plate than the front foot.
   - ✓ Weight a bit forward, toward plate, on balls of toes, a bit more on rear foot. Feel balanced in the legs.
   - ✓ Bend knees a bit, enough to feel loose.
   - ✓ Bend waist forward a bit.
   - ✓ Hands together, an inch from the end of the bat. Use a light bat.
   - ✓ Grip bat firmly, "feel" strength in the wrists.
   - ✓ Hands up, even with and slightly behind the rear shoulder, about 6 inches out.

✓ Bat points up and back a bit toward the catcher.

✓ Back elbow up, away from body, shoulders level (or front shoulder down a bit).

✓ Chin tucked into front shoulder, front shoulder tucked toward plate and down a bit.

✓ Be still. No dancing, no wiggling bat and no wiggling hips. Still, but not stiff.

5. The Swing.

✓ Get a good pitch, in the strike zone. See the ball immediately in front of you.

✓ Step into the pitch, toward the pitcher, while driving off the back toe.

✓ Swing level, almost coming down on ball, never uppercut. Keep head and front shoulder down. Move hands directly at the ball.

✓ Don't hitch or wind up and cock the bat at beginning of swing. Hands are still, and the only movement is to the ball directly.

✓ Open the hips with power, but not too soon.

✓ Extend the arms, whipping the head of the bat through the ball.

✓ Hit through the ball and follow through.

✓ Consider pitching on one knee, so the ball does not drop from too high.

✓ Have your batters switch hit, taking a few pitches from the opposite side.

6. Bunting.

✓ Turn and face the pitcher squarely as he releases the ball.

✓ Slide top hand along the bat about one-third to one-half the distance, cradling the bat head between the thumb and next finger. The left hand can travel toward the middle also, if it helps bat control and does not undermine grip.

✓ Keep the head of the bat high, coming down to the ball.

✓ Let the ball hit the bat, guiding the ball down the third base line.

✓ Spring from the batter's box immediately upon contact.

✓ Don't look at the ball, just run like the dickens.

# FIELDING

1. Catching.

✓ Have a catch. It's fun. Do it regularly.

- ✓ Quickly get under pop-ups, catch the ball above the head, fingers up, palms out, in the web of the glove. Use both hands. Err on the side of being too deep; it's easier to run in than it is to backpedal. If you must run back, turn and run instead of running backwards. Use a rubber ball at first.
- ✓ Get in front of grounders, spread legs, get glove down, bend knees, body low, weight forward, scoop ball into gut, hands soft, challenge ball affirmatively. Don't come up too soon, keep head down.
- ✓ Get a decent glove; this is critically important. Take care of it.

2. Throwing.
- ✓ Repetition is key. Have a catch.
- ✓ Push off same foot as throwing arm.
- ✓ Get set and balanced.
- ✓ Point other foot and shoulder at target.
- ✓ Reach back and extend arm with throw.
- ✓ Grip ball with two fingers on top. Ball shouldn't be too far back in palm.
- ✓ Look at target's glove, throw as level as possible. Throw hard unless target is close, then throw underhand.
- ✓ Outfielders should never hold the ball. Throw it in to cutoff immediately.
- ✓ Throw ahead of the lead runner, to the cutoff.

3. Rundowns.
- ✓ Get the runner to commit first.
- ✓ Run the runner back to prior base.
- ✓ Hold ball high, faking throw.
- ✓ Receiving fielder inside of base. Tag low.
- ✓ Other fielders back up fielders in the rundown.

## RUNNING AND SLIDING

1. Running Bases.
- ✓ Find a position that fits your player's speed.
- ✓ Run wind sprints to strengthen legs.
- ✓ Run on the balls of the toes, head and shoulders forward, arms churning.
- ✓ Know where the ball is at all times, always try to anticipate the

chance to advance to the next base.

✓ Plant left foot on inside of base and lean into the turn (either foot is OK).

✓ Try to draw the throw, fake advancing to next base, make things happen, get people's attention.

2. Sliding.

✓ Practice on a large piece of cardboard, no shoes.

✓ Right leg tucked in under the left.

✓ Slide flat on the butt, avoid turning on side.

✓ Stay low, flat, low, flat, low, flat.

✓ Don't break fall with the hand.

✓ Slide away from the ball.

## BASEBALL POSITIONS

1. Catcher.

✓ For gutsy kids or slower players. Get used to the crouch, on toes, squatting, not on one knee.

✓ Don't get too far back from the plate.

✓ Let the ball come to the glove, fingers up if high, down if low, hands soft.

✓ Free hand behind the back. Fist clenched.

✓ Control the pitcher, slow him down, keep him loose and strong and focus him on your glove.

✓ Look for fielders out of position.

✓ Block pitches in the dirt.

✓ Practice "quickness" on steals—retrieve ball, snatch and fire in one motion.

✓ Tag at plate low, block plate, helmet off, two hands.

✓ Practice foul tips.

2. First Baseman.

✓ Great for lefties, tall kids.

✓ Get to bag quickly, touch bag with foot opposite glove hand.

✓ Don't stretch for ball until you see path of throw, then stretch to meet it.

✓ Go get bad throws, leave the base if necessary.

✓ Practice throws in the dirt (wear catcher's gear if available).

✓ Go for balls in the hole.

✓ Lob to pitcher, show her the ball, lead her slightly.

✓ Practice foul pops.

✓ Once the runner has second base, move into the infield area to help out.

3. Second Base.

✓ Good glove, quick, does not need arm strength.

✓ Stay low, weight forward, eye on the ball to the hands, stay under the ball and scoop it out in front.

✓ Know where you are going to throw the ball.

✓ Cutoff on outfield balls to right side.

✓ Pivot man on double plays.

✓ Primary receiver on infield pop-up to right side.

✓ Cover first base on bunts to right side.

✓ Back up shortstop on steals.

4. Shortstop.

✓ Good glove, strong arm, leader.

✓ Play deep in the hole.

✓ Stay low, weight forward, eye on the ball to the hands, stay under the ball and scoop it out in front.

✓ Practice quick transition from catch to throw.

✓ Cut off for left side of outfield, or on any play to third base.

✓ Primary receiver on infield pop-ups, can call off anyone.

✓ Hold runners on third base on grounders before throwing to first base.

✓ Straddle the bag low on tags, especially steals, glove down.

5. Third Base.

✓ Good learning place, not a great deal of action, but need a strong arm.

✓ Need to make plays on steal, must stop the ball primarily, then tag low.

✓ See FIELDING, and other infield positions.

6. Outfield.

✓ Most action is to the right side, right fielder needs to have strongest arm.

✓ Run quickly to the ball, get there first instead of timing the run to meet the ball. Get under it quickly.

✓ If possible, hands high, palm outward, two hands.

✓ Don't hold the ball, throw immediately to the cutoff.

✓ Use rubber balls for practice at young ages.

✓ Block outfield grounders, lower body to one knee.

✓ Back up base in front of you on steals, especially left fielder.

7. Pitcher.

✓ Don't practice too much, arm will burn out, be sure to get rest.

✓ Start from same spot and position, consistency is key.

✓ Grip ball with fingers, ball away from palm, address batter, hands at side, take a breath.

✓ Rock the body and begin the windup.

✓ Lift front knee straight up, hands overhead, look at strike zone.

✓ Reach straight back with ball, kick front leg out toward batter, stretch, drive hard with back leg, lunge towards batter, whip open the left shoulder, extend the throwing arm, keep elbow up, snap wrist and throw over the top, open up hips and come down flat but hard with front foot in same place every time, follow through gracefully. These are separate moves, but all flowing together.

✓ Consistency, gracefulness, smoothness, confidence are keys.

✓ Take your time, don't rush in between pitches, get into a rhythm.

✓ Know your batters, challenge them, throw strikes.

✓ Cover first base on grounders to the first base side.

✓ Come home on wild pitches or passed balls.

Sometimes at a baseball game you think you are in a different country with the jargon. Here are some terms so you can "talk baseball" as well as anyone. Some things have been described in the body of the book, so there is no need to repeat them here.

**Appeal:** When a runner leaves a base too soon, does not tag up on a fly ball, misses a base when running; or when a batter swings the bat breaking the wrist with a ball called, a fielder may claim this violation and request the umpire's judgment. If the ump saw it, he will make the appropriate call—out, strike, return to base, etc.

**Backstop:** The fence that partially encloses the batter's box from behind. It usually is tall enough to keep foul tips from going too far back and hitting your car, although some do get past the fence and the cheers will indicate if a car gets hit. When you do batting practice it's good to have something tall behind the batter to stop the ball. It saves a lot of chasing time. I've used a piece of plywood or a large cardboard box if there is no backstop.

**Balk:** I've never seen this called in Little League play, but it's in the rule book. A balk is the penalty for the pitcher faking a pitch to get a base runner off balance. I guess since there is no stealing until the ball reaches the batter, the main thing a balk is supposed to eliminate can't happen anyway. If the pitcher is on the rubber and makes any motion indicating the beginning of the pitch, or feigns a throw to a base, the runners are all allowed to advance one base. It is also a balk if the pitcher does not come to a complete stop between his windup and the pitch. In 1988 umpires started calling this in the major leagues and it led to a period of much confusion.

**Ball:** A pitch outside of the strike zone. Four balls in one at bat entitle the batter to go to first base, called a "walk."

**Base bag:** There are three of them, one at each corner of the infield. While on base the runner can't be tagged out, unless he was forced to advance. The fourth base is called "home plate."

**Batter's box:** A 3-foot by 6-foot box on either side of the plate, starting 27½ inches behind the back tip of the plate, and coming up four inches from the side of the plate. The batters must be entirely inside the box while hitting the ball.

**Breaking ball:** A pitch that carries a lot of spin designed to make it curve or break direction as it travels toward the batter, making it necessary for the batter to adjust the swing accordingly. The ball breaks because the spin creates greater pressure on the part of the ball that spins forward. On a fastball the bottom of the ball spins forward so the ball rises. I rarely hear of kids being taught to throw a curve, slider, knuckleball, sinker, hook or other breaking pitch. The word is that a kid can hurt his arm snapping his wrist if he does it wrong. The rules don't prohibit it, but I've seen umpires tell the kid to stop. I remember one kid who had a natural curveball; he didn't know he was throwing one. I had to explain to the ump that it's not an illegal pitch, and besides the kid couldn't stop it.

**Bullpen:** A separate section in foul territory where the pitchers sit in the big leagues. It's near where they warm up in case they get called in. I'm not sure why it needs to be so separate, but pitchers are often pretty flaky, so leave 'em there.

**Catch:** OK, we probably all know what a catch is. But the rule is that you have to possess the ball long enough to prove complete control of the ball. If you catch it squarely and then fall and dislodge the ball, it's not a catch. Different kinds of catches include a basket catch, over the shoulder, diving and backhand. A catch is also called a *stab* and a *grab*. A ball that bounces just as a player catches it is called a *trap*. One that bounces just before a player catches it is a *short-hop*.

**Choke up:** Holding the hands farther up the handle of the bat, a few inches closer to the fat end. It makes the bat lighter and easier to control. Smaller players or players with two strikes should always choke up. Bat speed is important. It does however reduce power.

**Count:** The number of balls and strikes on a batter at any moment.

**Crane:** When a pitcher lifts his foot high in the air when he is about to pitch. It looks like a crane lifting its leg.

**Dead ball:** A ball out of play because play is suspended, such as a batter hit by a pitch, a runner hit by a batted ball, a ball that goes into the dugout or any other out of bounds area.

**Diamond:** A name given to the infield, outlined by the four base paths and roughly resembling a diamond.

**Double play:** When the defense gets two outs during one play. Usually when a runner is on first, and an infielder touches second and first base with the ball before both runners get there. These are force plays. Another double play often occurs when a fly ball is caught and the ball is thrown to a base before a runner can get back to tag up.

**Dugout:** The place where players sit while waiting to play. Usually in the big leagues it's an area with a bench, dug a few feet into the ground (it's cooler).

**Error:** The failure of a fielder to catch a ball that should have been caught with ordinary effort, or an errant throw resulting in prolonging the at bat or a runner's advance. Mistakes or slowness are not errors. An error is also called a *boot*, a *muff*, or *throwing the ball away.*

**Follow through:** In hitting or pitching, allowing the bat or the pitcher's hand to continue along its normal course after the hit or pitch occurs. It allows for more control and power in both activities.

**Force play:** When a runner must advance on a batted ball because all bases behind her are filled with runners. For instance, if bases are loaded, everyone must reach the next base. If there are runners on first and second, both must advance to make room on first for the batter. A runner on first only must get to second to make room for the batter. The forced runner is out if a fielder with the ball touches a base the runner must advance to before the runner gets there.

**Forfeit:** A game that is won or lost by a call of the umpire for certain violations, such as failure to place nine players in the field, delay of game, or a persistent rule violation.

**Foul:** A foul ball is a batted ball that lands in foul territory. The foul territory is the area outside of the two foul lines. The foul lines run along the first and third baselines and extend out to the boundaries of the field, usually a fence.

**Fungo:** An extra thick bat used for hitting grounders or fly balls for defensive practice. It makes it easier to hit the ball. Remember, I recommend just throwing the ball for accuracy. It's tough to hit consistently for accuracy.

**Gamer:** A kid who really hustles and likes the game. Also, a game-winning hit.

**Grounder:** A ball that hits and travels or bounces along the ground in the infield.

**Ground-rule double:** A ball that bounces over the outfield fence or is touched by a fan after bouncing in fair territory. The batter advances to second base.

**Hit:** When a batter safely advances at least to first base on a batted ball that lands in fair territory. Hits are *singles, doubles, triples* or *home runs.* A home run with bases loaded (runners on each base) is a *grand slam.* A pop-up or fly ball is one hit up into the air. If it drops between the outfield and infield (shallow outfield) it is a *bloop* or a *Texas leaguer.* Hitting the ball is also called *sticking it, poking it, rapping it* or *nailing it.* A *line drive* is the most desirable hit, also called a *rope.*

**Inning:** The pro game is divided into nine innings. Youth baseball usually plays six or seven innings. An inning is played when each team has had a chance to bat. Once each team has made three outs in its half-inning, a new inning starts. If the score is tied after nine innings, the game continues until an inning ends with one team ahead.

**Interference:** Running into or obstructing a fielder trying to make a play; moving in a manner to hinder or distract a batter. In the first instance, the runner is out and other runners return to the last base they touched. The ball is dead. In the second case, the umpire warns the fielder to stop. If a fielder interferes with a runner, it is called *obstruction.*

**Lead:** When a runner takes a few steps toward the next base before the ball is pitched. This is not allowed in Little League play on the smaller fields for ages twelve and under. You cannot leave the base until the ball has reached the batter.

**Pitch:** We already talked about breaking balls. A hard straight pitch is a *fastball.* Another good pitch is a change of pace when the ball is thrown slowly after a normal windup. It confuses the batter who starts to swing too early, then suddenly has to slow down to wait for the ball. It is a pitch that is often said to "screw the batter into the ground." A ball thrown at a batter is a *beanball* or a *dust-off pitch.* At advanced levels, such pitching tactics are encouraged to get a batter worried or distracted. It's an unfortunate fact of life at that level. A pitch that can't be caught is a *wild pitch;* if it can be caught but isn't, the catcher is charged with a *passed ball.* If the pitcher wets the ball, causing the ball to move erratically, it is illegal, called a *spitball*. Another way to get a ball to move is to scuff up a part of it so the scuff catches air as the ball spins. Joe Niekro was suspended in 1987 for ten days for carrying an emery board in his pocket to scuff the ball. The knuckleball or screwball is a pitch that can break several times or in any direction. When a pitcher raises his hands above his head just before pitching, it is a windup. Then he lifts his left foot (righty pitchers) into a crane position and drives himself towards the batter into a stretch. After releasing the ball his hand continues on a follow-through.

**Strike zone:** The area over home plate from the batter's knees to his armpits, when the batter is in his normal batting stance. If any part of a pitched ball passes through this area the batter is charged with a strike. Three strikes are an out. Strike zones often vary by umpires, and this is the source of most arguments in baseball.

**Tag:** Touching a runner not on base with the ball, or with a glove containing the ball.

**Warm-ups:** Exercises done before any athletic endeavor to slowly warm up or heat and extend muscles.

# ABOUT THE AUTHOR

Jack McCarthy, like many Americans, is a sports enthusiast and has played and coached numerous sports all of his life. As a parent, he knows that athletic competition builds self-respect in young people. It also teaches them how to handle adversity and how to succeed. The Betterway Coaching Kids series was developed by Jack to help parents ensure that their child's experience in sports is a positive one.

Jack is an attorney and works for the New Jersey Courts. He lives with his wife and three children in Hillsborough, New Jersey. His other books in the series include titles on baseball, soccer, basketball and football. He has also written *Baseball's All-Time Dream Team*.

# INDEX

Martin, Billy, 120
Mattingly, Don, 19, 132
McGraw, Manager John, 116, 120
Morgenau, Eric, 118
Motivate, 110
Motivation, 120-124
  phrases, 123
Myopia, 133

**N**

No-pitch drill, 106, 107
Nutrition, 144, 145

**O**

Obstruction, 10
Ott, Mel, 19
Outahere drill, 104, 107
Outfield, 81-85
  abilities, 81
  backing up, 84
  cutoffs, 82, 83
  drills, 105
  fielding grounders, 83, 84
  practices, 81

**P**

Parents, 1, 2, 15, 16, 32, 33, 38, 39, 46, 58,
  66, 95, 127-130
  behavior at games, 129
  checklist of things to say, 123, 129, 133
  get kids interested, 128
  how to handle, 127
  interfering, 127
  pitching to your child, 32, 33
  playing time, 32
  positive attitude, 117
  problems with coaches, 2, 117, 130
  vision therapy, 133
Passed ball drill, 104, 107
Peak performance, 124-127
Pepper, 34, 104, 107
Pierce, Mary, 118
Pitch, 158
Pitcher, 85-93
  arm burnout, 86, 87
  drills, 104, 106, 109
Pitches, types of, 93
  age for curveballs, 93
Pitching
  grip, 90
  strategy, 92-93
  style, 87-89
  tips, 90
Pop-up drill, 103

Pop-ups, 39-42
Positions, 66-93
  catcher, 66-70
  first base, 80-83
  outfield, 81-85
  pitcher, 85-93
  second base, 73-76
  shortstop, 76-79
  third base, 79-81
Potential, player's, 101
Practice plans, 110-114
Practices, 94-114
  agility drills, 96
  batting practice, 105, 106
  defensive practice, 102, 103
  drills, 103-110
  evaluate players, 101
  five key goals, 95-96
  individual skills, 102
  pitchers, 106, 109
  practice plan, the, 110-114
  speed improvement drills, 100
  team execution, 109, 110
  warming up, 96-100
Pre-game routine, 126
Push-ups, 97, 138

**Q**

Quick cali set, 96

**R**

Risser, Dr. William, 139
Robinson, Brooks, 81
Robot, the, 100
Rockne, Knute, 120
Rose, Pete, 19
Rotations, 135, 136
Rules of baseball, 3-12
Rundown drills, 104
Rundowns, 56-58
Running and sliding, 59-65
  position sketch, 64
  running bases, 60, 61
  signals, 61, 62
  speed, 69
Ruth, Babe, 132

**S**

Saccades, 132
Sapolsky, Robert, 125
Scrimmage, 109
Second base, 73-76
  cutoff, 75, 76
  double play, 75

# More Great Books
# for Coaching Kids!

Your influence as a coach or teacher can give children (both yours and others) the greatest gifts of all: strong self-confidence and high self-esteem. These books are full of helpful illustrations and step-by-step guides on how to nurture and encourage children as they strive for success in sports and the arts. Plus, the friendly, familiar tone of each book will help both you and the child have fun as you learn.

**Coaching Youth Football**—*#70303/$12.99/160 pages/75 b&w illus./paperback*

**The Parent's Guide to Coaching Baseball**—*#70076/$7.95/128 pages/paperback*

**The Parent's Guide to Coaching Basketball**—*#70077/$8.95/136 pages/paperback*

**The Parent's Guide to Coaching Tennis**—*#70243/$12.99/144 pages/144 b&w illus./paperback*

**The Parent's Guide to Teaching Skiing**—*#70217/$8.95/144 pages/70 b&w illus./paperback*

**The Parent's Guide to Coaching Soccer**—*#70079/$12.99/136 pages/122 photos/paperback*

**The Parent's Guide to Coaching Hockey**—*#70216/$12.99/176 pages/65 b&w illus./paperback*

**The Parent's Guide to Teaching Self-Defense**—*#70254/$12.95/144 pages/250 b&w illus./ paperback*

**The Parent's Guide to Coaching Physically Challenged Children**—*#70255/$12.95/144 pages/ 15 b&w illus./paperback*

**The Parent's Guide to Camping With Children**—*#70219/$12.99/176 pages/20 color illus./ paperback*

**The Parent's Guide to Teaching Music**—*#70082/$7.95/136 pages/paperback*

**The Parent's Guide to Band and Orchestra**—*#70075/$7.95/136 pages/paperback*

# Dozens of Great Ideas to Help
# You Get the Most Out of Life!

**Raising Happy Kids on a Reasonable Budget-AS SEEN ON OPRAH WINFREY**—this one-of-a-kind guide is packed with dollar-stretching techniques and budgeting tips you need to raise happy and healthy kids—whether you have one child or ten! *#70184/$10.95/144 pages/paperback*

**Don Aslett's Clutter-Free! Finally and Forever**—Free yourself of unnecessary stuff that chokes your home and clogs your life! If you feel owned by your belongings, you'll discover incredible excuses people use for allowing clutter, how to beat the "no-time" excuse, how to determine what's junk, how to prevent recluttering and much more! *#70306/$12.99/224 pages/50 illus./paperback*

**Kids, Money & Values**—Packed with activities, games and projects! You'll have a lot of fun as you teach your kids good money management habits! *#70238/$10.99/144 pages/paperback*

**Holiday Fun with Dian Thomas**—A year-round collection of festive crafts and recipes to make virtually every holiday a special and memorable event. You'll find exciting ideas that turn mere holiday observances into opportunities to exercise imagination and turn the festivity all the way up—from creative Christmas gift-giving to a super Super Bowl party. *#70300/$19.99/144 pages/paperback*

**Make Your House Do the Housework, Revised Edition**—Take advantage of new work-saving products, materials and approaches, to make your house keep itself in order. You'll discover page after page of practical, environmentally friendly new ideas and methods for minimizing home cleaning and maintenance. This book includes charts that rate materials and equipment. Plus, you'll find suggestions for approaching everything from simple do-it-yourself projects to remodeling jobs of all sizes. *#70293/$14.99/208 pages/215 b&w illus./paperback*

**Families Writing**—Here is a book that details why and how to record words that go straight to the heart—the simple, vital words that will speak to those you care most about and to their descendants many years from now. *#10294/$14.99/198 pages/paperback*

**Stephanie Culp's 12-Month Organizer and Project Planner**—This is the get-it-done planner! If you have projects you are burning to start or yearning to finish, you'll zoom toward accomplishment by using these forms, "To-Do" lists, checklists and calendars. *#70274/$12.99/192 pages/paperback*

**How To Get Organized When You Don't Have the Time**—You keep meaning to organize the closet and clean out the garage, but who has the time? Culp combines proven time-management principles with practical ideas to help you clean-up key trouble spots in a hurry. *#01354/$10.99/216 pages/paperback*

**Slow Down and Get More Done**—Discover precisely the right pace for your life by gaining control of worry, making possibilities instead of plans and learning the value of doing "nothing." *#70183/$11.95/192 pages/paperback*

**You Can Find More Time for Yourself Every Day**—Professionals, working mothers, college students—if you're in a hurry, you need this time-saving guide! Quizzes, tests and charts will show you how to make the most of your minutes! *#70258/$12.99/208 pages/paperback*

**Writing Family Histories and Memoirs**—From conducting solid research to writing a compelling book, this guide will help you recreate your past. Polking will help you determine what type of book to write, why you are writing the book and what its scope should be. Plus, you'll find writing samples, a genealogical chart, a publication consent form, memory triggers and more! *#70295/$14.99/272 pages*

**Streamlining Your Life**—Tired of the fast-track life? Stephanie Culp comes to the rescue with quick, practical, good-humored and helpful solutions to life's biggest problem—not having enough time. You'll get practical solutions to reoccurring problems, plus a 5-point plan to help you take care of tedious tasks. *#10238/$11.99/142 pages/paperback*

**Confessions of an Organized Homemaker**—You'll find hundreds of tips and ideas for organizing your household in this totally revised and updated edition. Discover motivation builders, consumer product information and more! *#70240/$10.99/224 pages/paperback*

**Conquering the Paper Pile-Up**—Now there's hope for even the messiest record keeper! You'll discover how to sort, organize, file and store every piece of paper in your office and home. Plus, you'll get instruction on how to deal with life's most important documents! *#10178/$11.95/176 pages/paperback*

**The Organization Map**—You WILL defeat clutter and disorganization. This clear, effective and encouraging guide is chock full of tips and advice for time-management, practical storage solutions and more! *#70224/$12.95/208 pages/paperback*